ARDAN APPLIED THE LIGHTED MATCH.

SURVIVAL SCRAPBOOK 3

ENERGY

Stefan A. Szczelkun

SCHOCKEN BOOKS • NEW YORK

TITLE

RITES

"A Squatters Mantle-Piece, Basset Street, Kentish Town, 1972-3"

First SCHOCKEN EDITION 1974
Published in cooperation with Unicorn Bookshop Brighton/Seattle
Library of Congress Catalog Card No. 73-82211
Copyright©1973 Stefan A. Szczelkun
Manufactured in the United States of America

ENERGY is the the capacity to do work...........?

Life on Earth derives its energy from the Sun, a vast incandescent ball of gas in which the nuclear transformation of hydrogen to helium gives off electromagnetic radiation.

Photosynthesis is the process by which a tiny fraction of this radiation is used with water and carbon dioxide to create organic matter, with the release of oxygen, in green plants.

$$6 CO_2 + 6 H_2O + sunlight \rightarrow C_6H_{12}O_6 + 6O_2$$

All forms of energy are interconvertible and when conversions occur they do so according to Laws of exchange. These are the Laws of Thermodynamics.

First Law : Within a particular system energy may be changed from one form to another but it is neither created nor destroyed.

Losses that seem to occur in energy transactions are due to the movement necessary. These losses are realised as heat which is a property of atoms in random movement or disorder. This is the subject of the,

Second Law : Processes involving energy transformations will not occur spontaneously unless there is a degradation of energy from a non-random to a random form.

Heat is a very special form of energy resulting from the random movement of molecules. It is evolved or less often absorbed when other forms of energy (which exist as the result of non random movement) are transformed.

AUTOVENT opens and closes the window automatically. No Power is needed! Bimetal strip magic.

Sketch of a sketch by Leonardo of a gas turbine for turning the spit.

One horse power = 1.34 Kwh   One Therm (100,000 B.th.U) = 29 Kwh   Kwh = Kilowatt hour.

Note on Units used. One Kwh = a one bar electric fire left on for one hour.

Power Output of Various **PRIME MOVERS**   in watts.

Man.............	50 — 100.
Horse............	500 — 750.
Wind + watermills....	2,500 — 20,000

WORLD ENERGY USE 1.

Heat 62% of total

Domestic	29%
Industry	33%

Power 38% of total

Domestic	2%
Agriculture	1%
Transport	19%
Industry	16%

1952 figures.

WORLD ENERGY USE 2.
per head of population.

Industrial West	— 116 — 246
Third World	— 9 — 30

in kilowatt hours per day.

Technocratic organization raises technical mediation to its highest point of coherence. It has been known for ages that the master uses the slave as a means to appropriate the objective world, that the tool only alienates the worker as long as it belongs to a master. Similarly in the realm of consumption: it's not the goods that are inherently alien- ating, but the conditioning that leads their buyers to choose them and the ideology in which they are wrapped. The tool in production and the conditioning of choice in consumption are the mainstays of the fraud: they are the mediations which move man the producer and man the consumer to the illusion of *action* in a real *passivity* and transform him into an essentially dependent being. The stolen mediations sep- arate the individual from himself, his desires, his dreams, and his will to live: and so people come to believe in the myth that you can't do without them, or the power that governs them. Where power fails to paralyse with constraints, it paralyses by suggestion: by forcing everyone to use crutches of which it is the sole supplier.

P.22. Revolution of Everyday Life. Part 2. by Raoul Vanetgem.

INFORMATION AREA

INFORMATION UNIT

forward facing   back facing

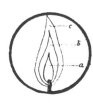

CONTENTS

INFORMATION AREA

INFORMATION UNIT

forward facing   back facing

STORAGE : HEAT.......STORAGE : MECHANICAL
STORAGE : ELECTRICAL..GAS CONVERSION.

ELECTRICITY GENERATOR...STEAM ENGINE
HEAT PUMP.............ALL TOGETHER
ALL TOGETHER.......STREET FARMHOUSE

ANIMAL POWER 1.....ANIMAL POWER 2.
HUMAN MUSCLE........DYNAPOD
MIND...................SIMPLE MEDITATION
REPRESSION...........CHI
BUREACRACY.........HYPNOSIS
C. M. I................MOB
DIE 1..................DIE 2
EFFICIENCY...........MISC.

MAPS INTRO...........SUN   U.S.
SUN   U.K..........WIND   U.S.
WIND   U.K........WATER   U.S.
WATER   U.K........HOT SPRINGS   U.S.
HOT SPRINGS U.K...WOOD   U.S.
WOOD   U.K.......FOSSIL   U.S.
FOSSIL   U.K.......COMPOSITE   U.S.
COMPOSITE   U.K...CONCLUSION.

BIBLIOGRAPHY 1....BIBLIOGRAPHY 2
BIBLIOGRAPHY 3....BIBLIOGRAPHY 4
BIBLIOGRAPHY 5....BIBLIOGRAPHY 6
BIBLIOGRAPHY 7....BIBLIOGRAPHY 8

CONTENTS

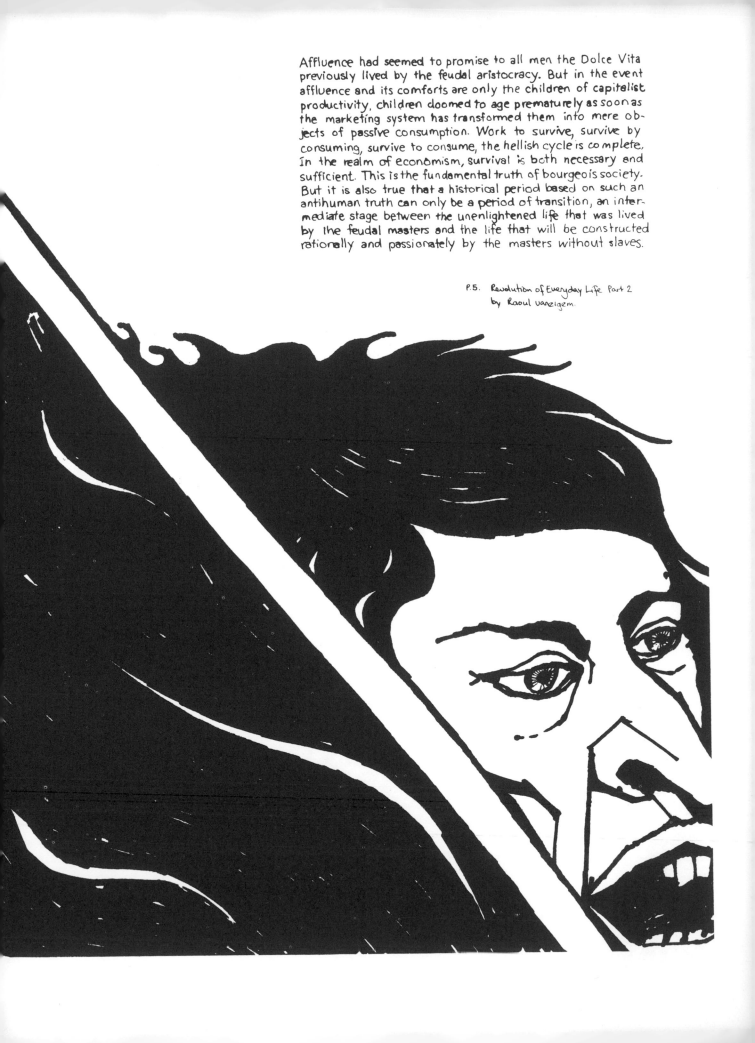

Affluence had seemed to promise to all men the Dolce Vita previously lived by the feudal aristocracy. But in the event affluence and its comforts are only the children of capitalist productivity, children doomed to age prematurely as soon as the marketing system has transformed them into mere objects of passive consumption. Work to survive, survive by consuming, survive to consume, the hellish cycle is complete. In the realm of economism, survival is both necessary and sufficient. This is the fundamental truth of bourgeois society. But it is also true that a historical period based on such an antihuman truth can only be a period of transition, an intermediate stage between the unenlightened life that was lived by the feudal masters and the life that will be constructed rationally and passionately by the masters without slaves.

P.5. Revolution of Everyday Life Part 2
by Raoul Vaneigem.

SUN POWER

North America is generally much sunnier than Britain, see map section, however even in the relatively dull temperate regions there are at least 1000 hours of sunshine per year, enough to make simple solar collectors worth while (Some collectors can make use of the diffuse solar radiation on cloudy days as well as direct sunshine.)

In regions where the sun shines only occasionally it may be used to power things that do not need a constant energy supply and are essentially intermittent activities that can 'wait' until the sunny spells. eg. solar distillation.

Electrical power generation from sun is at present feasible only in the sunniest areas. This does not stop you from being able to heat (or cool) a carefully designed (or converted) house solely by solar energy — — by careful use of double glazing north wall insulation, window shutters, controlled ventilation and a measure of storage — most places. Hot water can also be provided. This can all be done with the simplest low cost methods.

SUNLIGHT FALLING ON ONE SQ.M.				
MID. U.K.	latitude 52°	energy per square metre per day		YEARLY TOTAL
		MAX.	MIN.	
DIRECT		7.0	0.5	1400
DIRECT + DIFFUSE		8.4	0.8	1700

UNITS of power in kilowatt hours Kwh.
(one bar of an electric fire is usually one kilowatt.)

Printing Press Driven by Solar Energy. 1882.

Printing press driven by solar energy [1882]

SUN ONE

TYPES OF COLLECTOR

There are two main categories of collection device.

      1. The Flat-plate collector in which solar heat is absorbed into a flat surface. This type will pick up diffuse as well as direct sunlight.

      2. The Concentrator. In this type the sunlight is reflected and focused onto a small collection area.

ADVANTAGES OF FLAT-PLATE COLLECTORS OVER FOCUSING COLLECTORS.

1. They can more easily be made in the home workshop with simple materials.

2. Collect the diffuse radiation through clouds as well as direct sunlight. This is particularly important where periods of sunlight can rarely be relied upon.

3. Orientation to sun is not critical. Focusing collectors usually need a constant tracking mechanism so that they can 'follow' the sun.

4. May be used as part of the fabric of a building. For instance, the flat surface is easily adapted as a use- ful part of the roof.

5. Less maintenance is necessary. The reflective surfaces of a focusing collector need much care.

ADVANTAGES OF FOCUSING COLLECTORS

1. It is possible to achieve high temperatures. (for cooking or engines.)

2. Useful early morning and late afternoon as it can be orientated to gain full advantage of a low sun.

3. Can be very light weight (using a 'vacuum deposition of Aluminium on plastic) and may fold-up small.

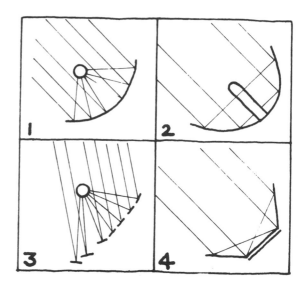

FOUR TYPES OF CONCENTRATOR.

Note. No.4 combines reflective panels with a flat plate collector.

SIX TYPES OF FLAT-PLATE.

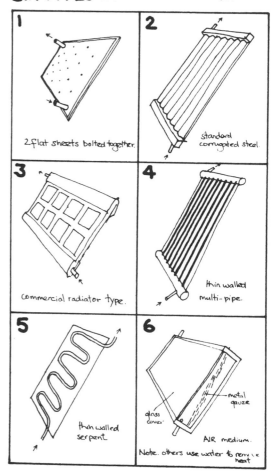

1. 2 flat sheets bolted together.
2. standard corrugated steel.
3. commercial radiator type.
4. thin walled multi-pipe.
5. thin walled serpent
6. metal gauze / glass cover / AIR medium. Note. others use water to remove heat

SIMPLE FLAT PLATE COLLECTORS
ESSENTIALS.

vent

hot water →

pipes slope continuously upwards and are lagged, as is the tank.

Tank approx. 20 gallons

glass cover

black surface

water 'radiator'

2/3 tank height.

50 cm. min.

Cold water supply at low pressure (ie gravity feed from tank with ball cock.)

tap to shut off circulation during cool periods and at night.

Angle = Latitude + 12°

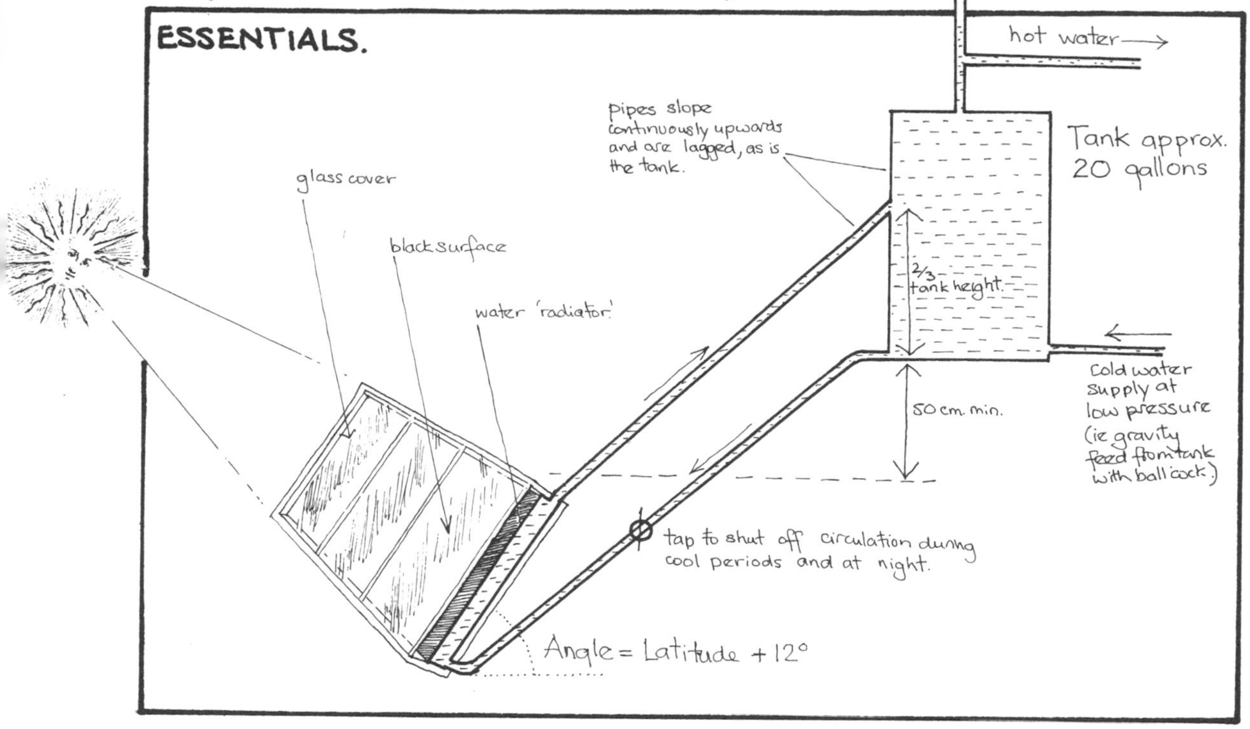

The simplest collector panels are like common domestic wall radiators. In fact discarded radiators may be used for the purpose. Otherwise you need to make a metal panel through which water can flow in some way. The water will absorb the heat gained by the surface facing the sun and as it gets hotter it will rise up through the panel and be lead off to a storage tank from an outlet at the top of the panel. (no pump is necessary as hot water rises through natural convection.)

The surface of the panel facing the sun is painted matt black as it is this color that is best at absorbing radiation. Ordinary hose piping or low pressure plumbing pipe may be used to join the outlet to the storage tank. This may be an old oil drum or galvanised water tank.

The pipe joins to the top of the tank with a simple inlet, which may be obtained at any store that holds a good range of plumbing supplies. The warmed water enters the tank about two thirds 'of the way up.' see diagram above. At the bottom of the tank an outlet leads relatively cool water down to the bottom of the collector plate. Tank and pipes must be well insulated with some common insulation material (see. SSI shelter.) to keep the heat in.

The water will keep circulating through this simple arrangement of collector and storage tank gradually getting hotter until it reaches the temperature of the surface of the collector (actually rather lower because of heat losses.)

Water may be drawn off for use at any time using a tap let into the tank. The water level must be kept topped up as water is removed.

FLAT PLATE COLLECTOR 1

SIMPLE FLAT PLATE COLLECTOR 2.

Orienting the collector directly towards the sun all day long is possible with a simple tracking device (eg. driven by clockwork.) However do not worry if you do not feel up to this, as you will get good results with a fixed, south facing collector; and morning and evening sun rays are not so hot.
It is worthwhile to fix the collector so that its face is perpendicular to the noon sunshine. The angle may be manually adjusted every month during the year as the sun becomes higher and lower in the sky.
These adjustements^{again} are not critical and a collector fixed on a fairly steep south facing roof will give good enough results.

Insulation of the back of the collector is important or else much heat will be lost to the surrounding air. (minimum of 1" polystyrene or 3" straw matt.) Heat losses will also occur on the sunward face of the collector and it is best to cover the front with transparent plastic or glass leaving about 1" air gap. This will help to trap heat in the system in a similar way that heat is trapped in a greenhouse.

Double and even triple layers of glazing have been tried but it is reckoned that as much heat is lost by reflection as is gained by the added insulation.

A tap to shut off the circulation at night is useful or else the process will reverse and all your gathered heat will be re-radiated to outer space from the cooling collector.

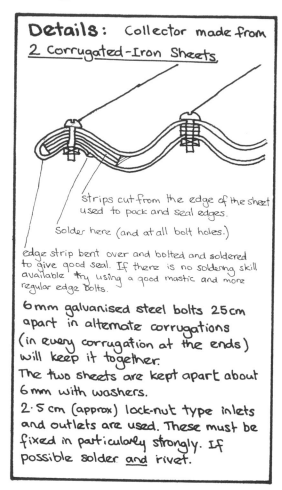

Details: Collector made from 2 Corrugated-Iron Sheets.

strips cut from the edge of the sheet used to pack and seal edges.

Solder here (and at all bolt holes.)

edge strip bent over and bolted and soldered to give good seal. If there is no soldering skill available try using a good mastic and more regular edge bolts.

6mm galvanised steel bolts 25cm apart in alternate corrugations (in every corrugation at the ends) will keep it together.
The two sheets are kept apart about 6mm with washers.
2·5 cm (approx) lock-nut type inlets and outlets are used. These must be fixed in particularly strongly. If possible solder _and_ rivet.

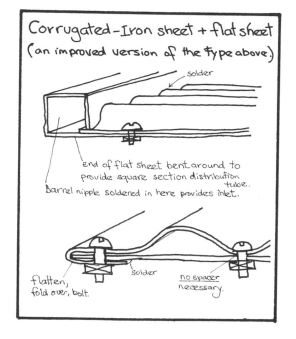

Corrugated-Iron sheet + flat sheet (an improved version of the type above)

solder

end of flat sheet bent around to provide square section distribution tube.
Barrel nipple soldered in here provides inlet.

flatten, fold over, bolt.

solder

no spacer necessary.

SIMPLE FLAT COLLECTOR 3.

The Storage Tank should be joined to the collector with the shortest connecting pipes possible for good circulation and low heat losses. The pipes should also be lagged to reduce heat losses. The tank should hold about 50 litres or 12 gallons per square metre of collector surface. Bigger collectors than approx. 3 square metres begin to suffer circulation problems.

The tank must be constantly full and this may be achieved from a ball cock cistern (the same as you get in a common W.C.) If your water supply is not pressurised you will need to pump water to fill the tank each time you draw water (hot!) off.

It is best to keep pipework design simple at first; at least until your first gush of piping hot solar heated water gives you sun-inspired energy for a more complex system. The two things to keep a look out for in pipework design are ——

    1. Prevention of air locks. As domestic water heats up it loses its dissolved air (up to 3%.) The air pockets thus formed will cause blockages unless you ensure the continuous upward slope of pipes to a vent pipe so that the air may escape.

    2. Reduction of flow resistance. esp. in the collector/tank circuit. This means keeping pipe runs as short and smooth (no sharp corners etc.) as possible.

To avoid the problems of intermittent water usage from the storage tank fit a simple heat exchange as shown at the top of the page.

To ensure hot water through cold spells the tank can have several secondary heating systems. eg. woodfire boiler, electric immersion heater, heat pump.

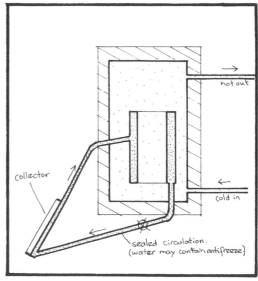

collector

hot out

cold in

sealed circulation. (water may contain antifreeze)

Secondary heating systems can also be used to __boost__ the temperature if it does not reach the required level. Another advantage of this system is that the water that circulates through the collector circuit can have anti-freeze added to avoid damage to the collector on frosty nights. Note. If you do not do this it will be nessary to drain the collector during winter nights, unless a pump system, in which the collector is mounted above the water level, allows the water to fall from the collector by gravity when the pump is switched off.

The pump may be of the type normally used for garden fountains; check it is O.K. for hot water and powerful enough to pump the head of water in your design.

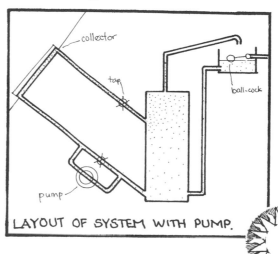

collector

tap

ball-cock

pump

LAYOUT OF SYSTEM WITH PUMP.

AIR MEDIUM FLAT COLLECTORS

Air may be used as a medium to carry heat away from a collector. Experiments have shown that several layers of very thin black painted expanded metal, arranged so that air flows through, (see right.) works very well. The expanded metal or gauze may be obtained ready to install or home-made by slitting and pulling out heavy grade aluminium foil.

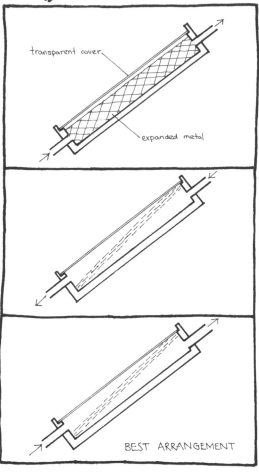

Three layers are reckoned to be most effective.

This is ideal for warm air space heating in a house as the added cost of heat exchangers, needed in a water medium system, is avoided.

Using air as a medium also gives possibilities of very lightweight collectors for use with vehicles and lightweight structures such as tents.

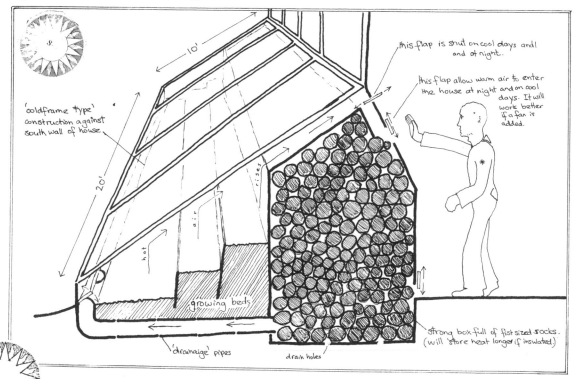

SOLAR PONDS

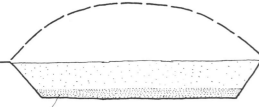

dissolved salts form a layer of strong brine over the black bottom of the pool.

1. Clean water is essential. The salt solution used could be one of magnesium chloride.

2. Depth of the pool is between one and two metres.

3. The salt solution prevents the usual convection currents causing heat loss from the bottom of the pool.

4. A cover for the pool could be a dome or similar lightweight structure clad in clear P.V.C. This would; — stop wind mixing the solution, keep the pool clean, added 'greenhouse effect'.

5. Heat must be extracted via heat exchanger so as not to disturb the pool.

6. Temperatures of up to 90°C! have been obtained in experiments.

7. I don't know if this works on a home-made level. Advantage is low cost, high temperature for big installation.

It comes from U.N. Conf. proceedings. Solar Energy.

A Couple More Crazy Ideas

With the advent of thin film super light weight plastics, and using the principle that hot air is lighter than cold air per unit volume.
Buck Fuller did a imaginative project years ago in which he proposed mile diameter geodesic spherical cities that could float around the earth. Their internal atmosphere was heated by the suns radiation; a few degrees rise in temperature is enough to give it lift.! Models of such structures have recently been found to work. A solar 'powered' hot air balloon is currently being tested. As the sun shines all the time above the clouds pollution free airships could soon replace jumbo jets.

(see Architectural Design Magazine. 5/73. pp. 267-8)

Heated 'Swimming Pool.'

The amount of heat per day required to raise the temperature of an open air swimming pool by 10°F is approx ½ kilowatt per day for each sq. ft. of surface area. An equal area of solar collector is necessary to give this rise. Normally such a large area of collector is out of the question in terms of 'cost' but if a south facing roof slope is available adjacent to the pool and of comparable area then a very cheap and simple collector may be made by using the roof surface.
On sunny days water is pumped to a ridge distribution trough from which it flows evenly down the roof to an eaves trough (gutter) which takes the water back to the pool via a suitable simple sand filter to remove dirt.
Roof surface should ideally slope at an angle slightly more than the latitude and should be of dark color. (black asbestos is good + cheap.) Thermal insulation below the roof surface is not needed as the pool temperature is usually slightly below the ambient air temperature. The water pump should be capable of delivering 200-300 gallons per hour for each 100 sq. ft. of roof surface available (wind pump?)
Improvements over the basic set-up would include covering the pool with a transparent structure and covering the roof (with plastic stretched directly over the tiles.) *mainly from a BRACE INSTITUTE leaflet.*

HOT PONDS

SOLAR STILLs

The solar still is simple to construct in many forms and is the safest and often the simplest way of purifying water. All kinds of sour and brackish water sources may be used to obtain drinking water. At present it is not feasible to distil seawater for agricultural use as it requires an area of still equal to cultivated area to give a minimum 'rainfall' equivalent. Stills are however used in particularly arid areas to provide up to 10 gallons per person per day for general use at reasonable cost!

This technology is, in fact, at least 100 years old being used in Chile, with economic success, to supply fresh water to the salt petre miners from brackish well source. Most solar stills used now are similar to the type used then.

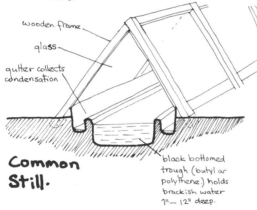

wooden frame
glass
gutter collects condensation

Common Still.

black bottomed trough (butyl or polythene) holds brackish water 7" — 12" deep.

Stills, like the cloche type arrangement above, heated water to 150°F and were efficient (about 35%) Improved designs may reach an efficiency of 60% but only with ideal conditions and will higher initial costs. Biggest loss is by reradiation from heated water. Other losses are from internal air circulation, reflection, absorption by glass cover, ground and edge losses, re-evaporation etc. (in approx. order of heat loss.)

<u>Plastic Stills</u> have the advantages over glass of less cost, lighter, less easy to break, easier to erect. However it is generally not as good as glass. The condensing water forms drops, that tend to fall back into the supply trough, rather than the even film that you get on glass. (reduces efficiency by roughly ⅓.) Care must also be taken that the plastic is tensioned over suitably sized frames or it will flap in the wind reducing its life span and production efficiency. A good method of construction for an 'occasional' still is ;—

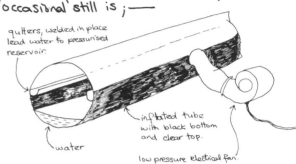

gutters, welded in place lead water to pressurised reservoir.

inflated tube with black bottom and clear top.

water

low pressure electrical fan.

Note: Farrington Daniels mentions that plastic film may be made more 'wet-able' by scratching over the surface with water proof grinding paper.

Simple Permanent Installation.

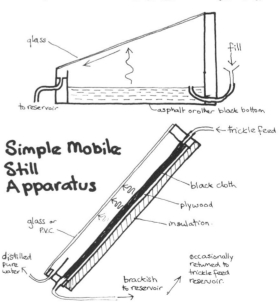

glass

fill

to reservoir

asphalt or other black bottom

Simple Mobile Still Apparatus

trickle feed

black cloth
plywood
insulation.

glass or P.V.C.

distilled pure water

brackish to reservoir

occasionally returned to trickle feed reservoir.

GREENHOUSE EFFECT

The major part of the solar radiation spectrum is in the wave lengths between 0.1 and 2.5 microns. Window glass and many transparent plastics are opaque to wavelengths much shorter or longer than this. Now, when the sun heats things behind glass they absorb the radiation and rise in temperature. They then re-radiate their excess heat. However the wavelength of the radiation emitted is longer than 2.5 microns, i.e. in the infra-red spectrum, and cannot escape through the glass which is opaque to radiation of this wavelength. This causes the temperature to rise and build up behind the glass.

This 'greenhouse effect' may be put to use in many ways and is an important consideration in the design of buildings.

Diagram of Richard the Squatlers Room Conversion.

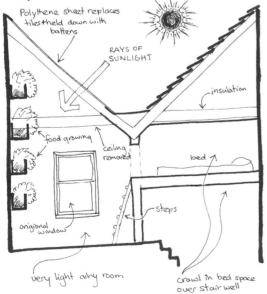

Polythene sheet replaces tiles+held down with battens

RAYS OF SUNLIGHT

insulation

food growing

ceiling removed

bed

original window

steps

very light airy room

crawl in bed space over stair well

Basset street, Kentish Town. 1973.

The simplest and least costly way to use the suns energy in house design is to orientate a great deal of the window area towards south, double glaze the windows and install insulated shutters. These shutters are closed at night so that the heat gathed during the day is kept inside at night. This combination of extensive areas of window, double glazing and shutters can cut heating power requirements in half, if you can stand the glare (actually this can be avoided by the use of baffles.) Possible disadvantage: you have to get up at dawn to open shutters if you want maximum effect.

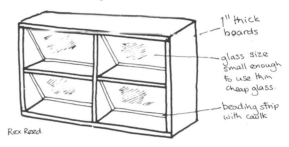

1" thick boards

glass size small enough to use thin cheap glass.

beading strip with caulk

Rex Reed

This is the way to make a cheap glass wall.

A thick rammed earth or rock wall (2'—3' minimum) may be used to absorb solar heat during the day, store it and reemit it at night. see below.

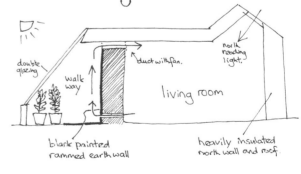

double glazing

walk way

duct with fan.

north reading light.

living room

black painted rammed earth wall

heavily insulated north wall and roof.

The ducts are closed during the day and opened at night when the shutters or metallised blinds are closed to insulate the windows. Air circulates by natural convection. Ken Kern.

FOCUSING COLLECTORS

High optical precision is unnecessary for producing temperatures in the neighbourhood of 500°C.

The simplest focusing collectors were made by cutting a circular hole 40" in diameter in a rectangle of reinforced plywood and stretching aluminised Mylar 1 mil. thick over the hole. A layer of cloth and burlap is stretched over the aluminised surface of the mylar and a heavy coating of liquid (polyester or epoxy resin) plastic is applied.

The frame is then inverted and supported at the edges while fine sand is poured onto the stretched mylar, causing it to sag. Over-night the plastic hardens and the sand is poured off. The catenary curve produced gives good enough focusing for use with a cooking vessel.

For more accurate focusing a mould must be made or found.

Note: Collectors of anything over 6ft. (2M.) in diameter tend to be unmanageable.

Disadvantage: time necessary to boil 2 litres on a sunny day = 30 minutes to 2 hours.

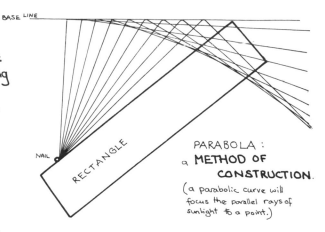

BASE LINE

NAIL

RECTANGLE

PARABOLA : a METHOD OF CONSTRUCTION.
(a parabolic curve will focus the parallel rays of sunlight to a point.)

Making a Parabolic Dish Mould.

Plywood knife edges of parabolic curvature are use to shape wet sand in a box by rotating them about a central pivot. Wet plaster is then carefully poured into the sand mould. A hollow plaster mould is made in this way. Removed from the sand it is smoothed until perfect.

This mould is then used to make a glassfibre (g.r.p.) dish onto which may be stuck small mirrors or 'orange peel' sections of metalised plastic.

Parabolic Mirror Cylinder
does not need tracking mechanism.

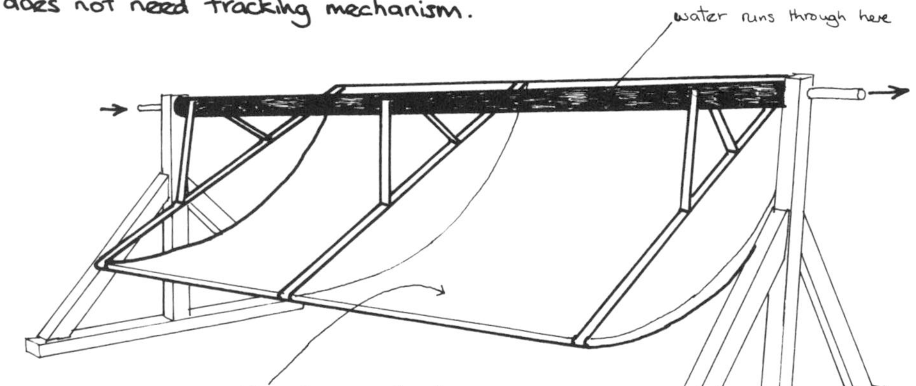

water runs through here

strips of mirror 1" wide laid onto ply or fibreglass mount

FOCUSING COLLECTORS 2

Sophisticated sun energy collecting devices that can do useful work were produced as long ago as 1878. The following description of an early machine comes from the Arizona Republican of February 14th 1901. It is of a sun powered pump on an ostrich farm in Pasadena.

"The unique feature of the solar motor is that it uses the heat of the sun to produce steam. As 'no fuel' is cheaper than any fuel, the saving to be effected by this device is evident. When the solar rays have heated the water in the boiler so as to produce steam, the remainder of the process is the familiar operation of compound engine and centrifugal pump. The reflector somewhat resembles a huge umbrella, open and inverted at such an angle as to recieve the full effect of the suns rays on 1,788 little mirrors lining its inside surface. The Boiler, which is 13'6" long is just where the handle of an umbrella ought to be. This boiler is the focal point where the reflection of the sun is concentrated. If you reach a long pole up to the boiler it instantly begins to smoke and in a few seconds is aflame. From the boiler a flexible metallic pipe runs to the engine house near at hand. The reflector is 33½ ft. in diameter at the top and 15 ft. at bottom. On the whole its appearance is rather stately and graceful, and the glittering mirrors and shining boiler make it decidedly brilliant.

In the morning the machine is thrown into focus by a few turns of a hand crank. In about an hour the gauge in the engine house indicates 150 lbs of steam pressure. ——

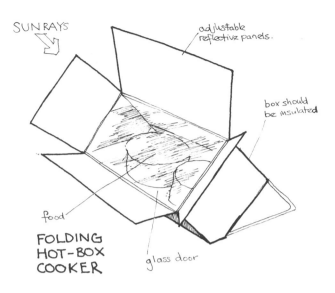

SUN RAYS

adjustable reflective panels.

box should be insulated

food

FOLDING HOT-BOX COOKER

glass door

Parabolic mirror

saucepan with black bottom

LIGHTWEIGHT SOLAR COOKER.

wheel hub allows adjustment for solar azimuth.

—The engine may then be started and allowed to run all day without attention. A clockwork arrangement keeps the reflector following the sun around automatically; the engine is self oiling; the water passes back from the condenser to the boiler so that the latter is always full. The present model runs a 10 horse power engine and lifts 1400 gallons per minute twelve feet from an underground tank."

quoted in 'the Coming Age of Solar Energy.'

Thermionic....... and   Thermo-electric devices

Thermionic converters use high temperatures (1500°C) to stimulate special surfaces to emit electrons to colder surfaces through a vacuum or atmosphere of positive ions. No materials are consumed but the emitter deteriorates after long usage, (cf. vacuum strip lights.) but long is estimated to be in the region of 10,000 – 50,000 hours.

Development of these converters is in early stages.

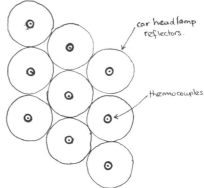

car head lamp reflectors.

thermocouples

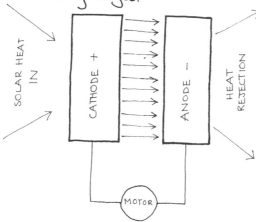

SOLAR HEAT IN

CATHODE +   ANODE −

HEAT REJECTION

MOTOR

A big disadvantage of thermionics for low-cost self build applications are the high temperatures involved which mean a high precision of manufacture of the solar focusing collector.

Although the thermionic converter is more efficient and theoretically more elegant than the thermo electric converter, the latter's comparative simplicity and lower cost gives it greater application at present.

'Thermo-electric refrigerators' were produced commercially in the U.S. in 1953 and the Soviet Union have apparently developed a generator of one horse power.

A thermocouple is made from 2 dissimilar metals in which the heating and cooling of alternate junctions produces an electrical potential. It is the device used in thermostatic switches and a full explanation may be obtained in any basic text book. (eg. 'How Things Work!')

"So simple is the solar battery that hundreds of youngsters have made their own using silicon wafers supplied by International Rectifier Company, chemically treating them and heating them in small furnaces"
"Bell Telephone Co. made available a complete kit for this purpose."
  so says Chang in "Energy Conversion".

I've never met any of these kids myself and cannot see any particularly urgent application of solar thermo-couples at present, but they sound neat so if you want to power your radio cheap on sunny days — you might investigate further.

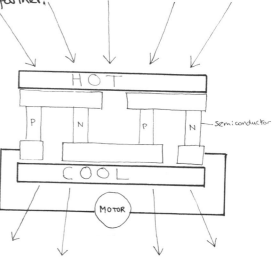

HOT

P   N   P   N   semiconductor

COOL

MOTOR

Solar Engines

"Small solar powered engines and generators can now be built for about $1000 per kw. of electricity produced compared with only $200/ kw. in large conventionally fuelled installations. But it looks as if costs will fall."

This is how Farrington Daniels summ- -arises the state-of-the-art in Sept. 1972 in Mechanical Engineering. He points out that many prototype solar engines using flat plate and focusing collectors and operating media such as steam, hot air and vapours of different kinds, have been built. The reason they are not generally available is because they are not 'economically viable' compared with standard fossil fuel powered internal combustion engines.

Small steam engines tend to be very inefficient but the small Stirling Hot Air Engine has good efficiency, has been developed over many years and can be built with a low capital investment.

Flat plate collector driven engines are limited to a temperature operation below 100°C which gives rather low efficiency but the large areas of collector possible with a low capital outlay mean large engines are possible.

Focusing collectors are more expensive limited to use on sunny days but are small in size and give high temperatures of around 500°C and are therefore more mobile and efficient. A 6ft diameter collector can operate an engine of up to 1/2 kw. power.

Farber at the Univ. of Florida has operated a 1/5 kw. Stirling hot air engine (made from a converted lawn mower engine.) He got 10% efficiency. A 1/5 kw. engine will give about 1/8 kw. of electricity which is equivalent to 2 60 watt bulbs.

The development of solar engines is obviously more for the mechanical wizards amongst us. It does seem their application in the British Isles would be very limited at present technological levels.

Note: For large engines perhaps the development of Solar Ponds will give the required heat.

See recent I.T.D.G. publication for more details.

"There are twenty-five exactly like this one."

SOLAR ENGINES

PRODUCTION OF COLD BY SOLAR HEAT.

A simple flat plate collector may be made to work in reverse at night and so provide summer cooling so long as a large heat/cold storage facility is available. e.g. a cellar full of rocks.

Proper refrigerating vapour cycles may be activated by a solar focusing collector. Of course this is more useful in arid/hot desert areas than in the British Isles, however it may find good use in the storage of food produce over long periods.

Power to produce cold being available at those times it is most needed. ie. in summer.

For more details + diagram see page on 'HEAT PUMPS' also see: How Things Work.

Portable absorption/desorption cooling units have been available for over 40 years and can be modified to be operated by solar heat.

The absorption/desorption cooler works on a similar principle to the heat pump. except that vapourisation is achieved through a reduction in pressure caused by a gas (eg ammonia) being absorbed into solution. Regeneration of the system occurs by heating the solution (solar) which releases ammonia vapour which is passed through a condenser before being reused.

F. Daniels reports on a basic home-made piece of refrigerating equipment in 'Direct Use of the Suns Energy_

"A 4' parabolic solar reflector focused sun heat onto a steel vessel containing ammonia and water. The ammonia was driven out with the heat and condensed in a small vessel connected by a steel tube or rubber hose capable of withstanding high pressures (ammonia reached over 10× atmospheric pressure or 150 lb in²)

The ammonia condensed in the small vessel which was cooled in a pail of water. After 4 hours exposure in bright sunlight the ammonia had all been driven out and had condensed.

The 2 vessel closed system which weighed about 25lb was taken into the house and the small vessel of liquid ammonia was put in an insulated box with a capacity of 2.2 cu.ft. When removed from the focused sunlight the water solution cooled and reabsorbed the ammonia. The evaporation of the liquid ammonia kept the box at below 5°C for twenty four hours."

Williams et al.

Intermittent absorption cooling systems with solar Refrigeration Eng. mag.   nov. 1958.   Regeneration.

Not enough detail for the uninitiated to build one from, unfortunately, but it does give some idea of what is possible.

note: Using this type of 'fridge John Harrison has achieved results by simply removing the heating element (or gas jet) and replacing it with a focusing collector!

VEG. SUN SCRAPS + Photosynthesis.

✳ The biggest world usage of solar energy is by green plants.

✳ One acre of ground can be expected to produce 3 tons of plant material per annum (dry weight.)

✳ In theory solar radiation provides enough energy (on a clear day) for the conversion of about 3 tons PER DAY. Improvements in 'efficiency' may be made by using a 3 dimensional growing medium. For example Chlorella algae production yeilds may be 20 tons per acre per annum.

✳ Todays 'efficiently' mechanised farming requires one calorie of (fuel) energy to produce one calorie of food (energy).   absurd?

✳ "A soybean soup called 'miso' is a staple breakfast item with Japanese, and _algae_ have been mixed with it one part in eight." (the factory infiltrate macro biotic food folks – oh yes!)

Mostly in this column from The coming Age of Solar Energy. Halacy Jnr.

"Under natural conditions on grazing land 5% only of the incident visible light is converted into the chemical energy of plant protoplasm and it is clear that animals in building up their body tissues which serve as food for man, dissapate a large proportion of the chemical energy of plant protoplasm as heat. Thus for man to make maximum use of the solar energy trapped by plants he should become _mainly_ herbivorous."

"Given good soil structure ample nutrients and water many natural ecosystems utilise fully the available incident solar radiation. This becomes possible when there is a full photosynthetically active plant cover throughout the growing season, and often throughout the year, which traps the maximum amount of sunlight, a condition rarely achieved with agriultural crops. One has only to think of the bare patches of earth between young crop plants to realise that much solar radiation of potential use in photosynthesis, is wasted. There are technical difficulties of planting and harvesting to overcome but there is a case for the growing of mixed crops, which together give a full plant cover." John Phillipson _Ecological Energetics_

GROWHOLE BASICS

1 THE SUN IS A SOURCE OF FREE ENERGY 2 THE EARTH STORES HEAT

THESE TWO FACTS MAKE IT POSSIBLE TO GROW VEGETABLES/FRUIT IN WINTER

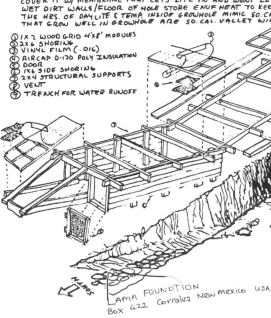

DIG A HOLE THAT FACES SOUTH TO CATCH AS MUCH SUNLITE AS POSSIBLE. COVER IT W/ MEMBRANE THAT LETS LITE IN AND WONT LET HEAT OUT. WET DIRT WALLS/FLOOR OF HOLE STORE ENUF HEAT TO KEEP WARM THRU NITE. THE HRS. OF DAYLITE & TEMP. INSIDE GROWHOLE MIMIC SO. CAL. VALLEY. PLANTS THAT GROW WELL IN GROWHOLE ARE SO. CAL. VALLEY WINTER CROPS.

① 1×2 WOOD GRID 4'×8' MODULES
② 2×6 SHORING
③ VINYL FILM (.016)
④ AIRCAP D-120 POLY INSULATION
⑤ DOOR
⑥ 1×6 SIDE SHORING
⑦ 2×4 STRUCTURAL SUPPORTS
⑧ VENT
⑨ TRENCH FOR WATER RUNOFF

25° SLOPE

SOUTH

LAMA FOUNDTION
BOX 422 Corrales New Mexico USA

ALCOHOL...

Imagine running an engine or cooking your food using the same alcohol that you drink. It's not only possible but has been done in the past and probably is still being done in some part of the world. Ethyl Alcohol, also know as grain alcohol, ethanol, industrial alcohol, or C_2H_6O, has a heat value of 84,000 B.T.U. per gallon as compared to 135,000 B.T.U. per gallon for gasoline. Alcohol also has an octane rating of 99.

Alcohol is obtained by fermentation and distillation of various organic materials such as wood, corn, potatoes, sugar cane and sugar beets. Wood presents an interesting possiblility since it is widely available in the form of scraps and sawdust and paper products. The following table taken from Avres and Scarlott shows the possible alcohol yields of several materials.

ALCOHOL YIELDS FROM VARIOUS MATERIALS

Material	gal./ton	gal./acre
wood	70	70
corn	84	89
potatoes	23	178
sugar cane	15	268
sugar beet	22	287

Alcohol as a fuel in this and other countries is nothing new and has been used in wartime as well as promoted as a way to help farmers by growing crops for fuel. In the 30's and 40's the opposition of the oil industry to alcohol was very strong.

..........a few months later.

Some comments on the alcohol and wood gas article. Sugar from cane and beets can be fermented easily by the addition of yeast. The starch in potatoes also ferments readily if yeast is added. Corn should be sprouted first, then heated and ground before the addition of yeast, but once the right enzymes are present, ground unsprouted grain will ferment yielding ethyl alcohol.

The cellulose in wood is a different story. Cellulose must be hydrolyzed to glucose -- a fermentable sugar -- and this has been done industrially using strong acid, high temperatures, and high pressure, impractical methods for home use. Long boiling of sawdust in acid will convert the cellulose to glucose, but *an acid-resistant vessel is necessary*, and the acid should be neutralized and cooled before the addition of yeast.

Once the sugar has been fermented to alcohol (and carbon dioxide and water), the alcohol must be distilled out of the solution. The alcohol concentration can be as high as 16% if special strains of yeast are used, but 12% is more common. Ethyl alcohol boils at 78 C and water at 100 C, so it's necessary to heat the fermented solution in a suitable container so that the alcohol boils off and condenses before the water comes over and dilutes it to such an extent that it will not burn.

When your still is in operation, collect everything that distills up to about 85 C. Don't distill too fast. Rapid drops are preferable to a steady gush of liquid. Be careful! Ethyl alcohol is inflammable and explosive when mixed with air.

Fermentation and distillation are simple procedures to master. But there is one fly in the ointment. As usual, it's the government. You must have a federal license to operate a legal still *even if you are producing alcohol for fuel* -- and licenses are not easy to come by. Even if you use a still to distill water, you must have a license.

After reading a number of detailed engineering articles on production of ethyl alcohol from wood, I'd say flatly that none of the commercial methods could be used at home for making a few gallons for fuel. Strong acids mean corrosion proof metals, the acids must be recovered in order to be economical and prevent pollution. High pressure means thickwalled expensive pressure equipment.

The only process that looks at all feasible is an in-efficient one. If white spruce chips are heated with 3% hydrochloric acid for 6 hours at 96F one can get about 20% yield of fermentable sugar instead of the 70% one can get in a high temperature-high pressure process. This method just might be done in a 55 gal. drum with a heavy plastic liner.

Alcohol from wood usually contains several other substances which render it unfit for human consumption unless carefully purified. However, these substances can be used for fuel also.

If I had to have alcohol for fuel, I'd use potatoes, sugar beets or Jerusql beets or Jerusalem artichokes (10-20 tons/acre) rather than wood.

The table of alcohol yields quoted in ASE #8 gives 70 gal/ton as yield from wood. The theoretical amount is 94.1 gal/ton but none of the articles I've seen get more than 25-30 gal/ton.

Liquid hydrogen fluoride was proposed in 1933 for cellulose hydrolysis since it caused instant results at atmospheric pressure and 20-25C. It was not used commercially because there were few methods for handling hydrogen fluoride then. Today it could be done and the acid is easily recoverable since it is easily vaporized and condensed.

Lab yields of sugar from wood have been 85-90% and this method would seem to have promise. Perhaps we could solve part of our solid waste problem, converting old newspapers to alcohol.

For more information, see WOOD CHEMISTRY by Louis Wise, Reinhold Co, 1949.

Alcohol, cont.

The process of making fuel alcohol is no different from making high-proof moonshine. You need a mash to ferment, a still, and a smokeless heat source.

The mash can be made from anything which contains enough sugar or starch for yeast to convert to alcohol:

wood chips	sugar beets
fruit	refined sugar
potatoes	sugar cane
corn	corn stalks
oats	molasses
wheat	stale bread

All these come to mind as possible sugar and starch sources for the mash. You can use any one, or mix these materials in the final mash. The starchier sources, such as corn, potatoes, wood, etc., should be cooked for a few hours. The sugar sources shouldn't be heated too much. Toss everything together in a large container of warm water to make a soupy mash. Add yeast and cover with a cloth. If your temperature is around 70 F your mash should be 10% alcohol at the end of two weeks. At this point it is ready for the still.

The traditional still is made of copper throughout -- a precaution against metallic impurities in the final product (and in its consumer). A still for fuel alcohol could be put together out of old oil drums and copper tubing.

A warning! The alcohol from this set-up will NOT be fit to drink! A drink of it could kill you -- just like a drink of gasoline. If you really want to ruin your head on the same juice that runs your tractor, then read John F. Adams' *An Essay on Brewing, Vintage, and Distillation*, Doubleday, 95¢. The book has an excellent discussion on stills in general.

Heat your mash in Barrel "A" to 170 - 180 F, above the boiling point of alcohol but below that of water. Alcohol steam rises and travels through ½" tubing to condenser barrel "B", through which is a 10-foot coil of copper tubing, and which is filled with cold water. Alcohol trickles out of the end of the tube into your waiting container. The batch is finished when the trickle from the tube turns to water, and you'll see that the liquid changes

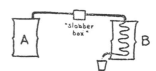

consistency quite markedly.

If you add a "slobber box" between the primary vat and the condenser, you'll get a purer product. The slobber box allows fewer volatile gases to condense and thus be removed from the distillate. But you should run everything through twice for the cleanest-burning alcohol.

The spent mash will re-ferment when yeast is added, increasing your yield by 50%. If the mash still seems sweet, you can keep on re-fermenting after each distillation, till the sugar and starch are all gone.

Questions: Does anybody out there know the legal aspects of distilling your own fuel alcohol? Will my old John Deere actually run on it? (It runs on regular gas or diesel fuel.) How about running a regular car? A Briggs & Stratton engine? A Coleman stove or lamp? I would mightily like to know the answers to these.

John Cuddy
Sunflower Farm
RR 2
Shevlin, MN 56676

Phil Carabateas
2008 Kingman Rd.
The Brier Patch
Nassau, N.Y. 12123

ALCOHOL

cut from
A.S.E.
Alternative Sources of Energy magazine
cost..... (send $1.) from Don Marier (editor) Route 1 Box 36B Milaong
Wisconsin 54 859. U.SA.

WIND

...is possibly the best free energy source in the north East of America + British Isles. There are few places where some kind of wind driven machine will not be of use; but of course open windswept places are far better than sheltered valleys.

The map gives some overall idea of where the wind blows most. Local conditions can effect the available wind power potential greatly. The increase of wind speed with height is a well recognised phenomena. How much. tall towers are justified is a complex economic point but it is generally not worth building towers of more than 50 foot unless a supply of suitable material is available. As much use of the local topography must be made as is possible, avoiding turbulent spots and finding the highest and most exposed places that have a natural wind funneling effect.

Accurate and detailed wind speed measurements are, however, only necessary for the more sophisticated and larger windmills rather than the 'run of the mill' homemade machine.

left: test of prototype Madaras rotor, Burlington, new Jersey. 1933.

A 2 blade turbine of 6 foot diameter will equal the human output of work in a moderate 10 m.p.h. breeze.

SMOOTH HILL. WINDS SPEEDS UP NO TURBULENCE.

ROUGH COUNTRY TURBULENCE NEAR TO GROUND.

The power that exists in kinetic form in a current of air of cross-section A is ;——
Power = K × A × V³
(usable)

*K = constant of efficiency . 0·6
V = wind speed.

POWER AT A GLANCE in watts

WIND VELOCITY in M.P.H.							
5	0·6	1	2	4	5	10	15
10	5	11	19	30	42	75	120
15	16	36	64	100	140	260	400
20	38	85	150	240	340	610	950
25	73	160	300	410	660	1180	1840
	2	3	4	5	6	8	10

DIAMETER OF MILL IN feet. (2 blade high speed type)

Thanks to Ed Trunk + Mother Earth News 17.

WIND ONE

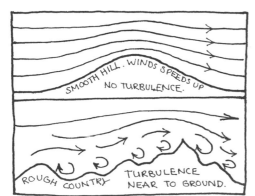

Preliminary Notes:

Wind Measurements on a site are of 3 classes. 1. Long term measurements to determine possible power output. 2. Medium term to establish wind structure in various weather conditions to enable a choice of wind unit. 3. Short term to determine detailed mechanical characteristics esp. with respect to gusts.

Apart from average wind velocities an important measurement is the maximum wind speed which determines the stresses that must be withstood by the machine.

Much valuable information on wind speeds and directions already exists in the records of national meteorological services, although these are general and do not take interest in the most exposed windiest sites. Uses are.

i) Areas of highest wind speeds.

ii) Direction of prevailing wind.

iii) Measure of constancy, or variability of year to year wind speed.

iv) As an indication of the annual wind regime.

v) Measure of the maximum speeds and duration of calm spells.

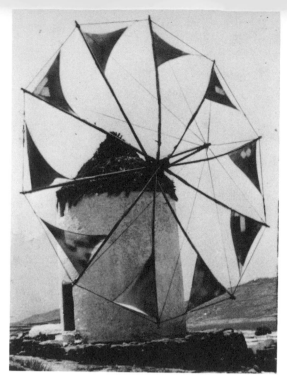

photo courtesy of the Museum of English Rural Life, Univ. of Reading. Shows mediterranean type mill with adjustable sails.

Note: SAFETY WARNING DANGER

Great care must be taken with home-made wind machines near habitation, especially in towns, on account of their persistent habit of disintegrating at high speeds and showering a wide area with a deadly shrapnel of windmill parts. Test your machine thoroughly in hurricanes out of harms way. Always turn off machines when you are not around unless a <u>foolproof</u> automatic governing and cut-out device has been attached.

❊ **Sails are safest.**

❊ 2½" ordinance Survey maps show wind pumps like this: Wd.Pp. Even if they don't exist now there may be old bits in the barn or old folks with useful memories. Investigate.

❊ Wind speeds are likely to be higher in winter than summer......which is useful.

HOLLANDSCHE MOLENS   WIND MILLS

At one time there were over 12,000 mills operating in Holland — average output 8 h.p.

CLASSIFICATION of WINDMILL TYPES.

GENERATOR
FURLING PUSH ROD
LUCAS Freelite
FURLING FLANGE
TAIL BOOM
TAIL VANE
CLAMP
GUY WIRE ATTACHMENTS
STEEL STEPS
FENCING WIRE
EYELET
FURLING HANDLE
FURLING SPRING
NORMAL RUNNING POSITION

Construction of Lucas "Freelite" wind-driven generator 1940s

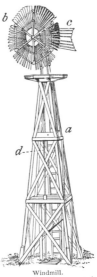

Windmill.
a, frame; *b*, sails; *c*, vane; *d*, pump-rod.

windmill (wind'mil), *n.* [< ME. *windmille, wind-melle, windmulle, windmilne, wyndemylne* = D. *windmolen* = MHG. *wint-mül,* G. *windmühle;* < *wind*^{2} + *mill*^{1}, *n.*] 1. A mill or machine for grinding, pumping, or other purposes, moved by the wind; a wind-motor; any form of motor for utilizing the pressure of the wind as a motive power. Two types of machines are used, the horizontal and the vertical. The vertical motor consists essentially of a horizontal shaft called the *wind-shaft,* with a combination of sails or vanes fixed at the end of the shaft, and suitable gearing for conveying the motion of the wind-shaft to the pump or other machinery. The older types of windmill used four vanes or sail-frames called *whips,* covered with canvas, arrangements being provided for reefing the sails in high winds. To present the vanes to the wind, the whole structure or tower carrying the windmill was at first turned round by means of a long lever. Later the top of the tower, called the *cap,* was made movable. Windmills are now made with many wooden vanes forming a disk exposed to the winds, and fitted with automatic feathering and steering machinery, governors for regulating the speed, apparatus for closing the vanes in storms, etc. These improved windmills are chiefly of American invention, and are largely used in all parts of the United States for pumping water. Horizontal windmills employ an upright wind-shaft, and movable vanes placed in a circle round it, the vanes feathering when moving against the wind.

> I saugh him carien a *wind-melle*
> Under a walshe-note shale.
> *Chaucer,* House of Fame,

Old Windmill at Bridgehampton, New York.

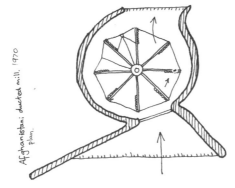

Lincoln, Nebraska 1890s

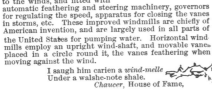

Hinged sails of canvas.   *Veranzio 1595*

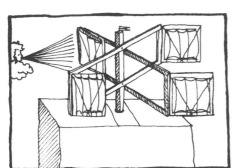

Afghanistani ducted mill. 1970
plan.

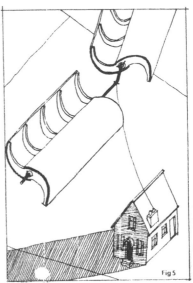

Fig 5   Stables Flying Rotor 1980s

TYPES

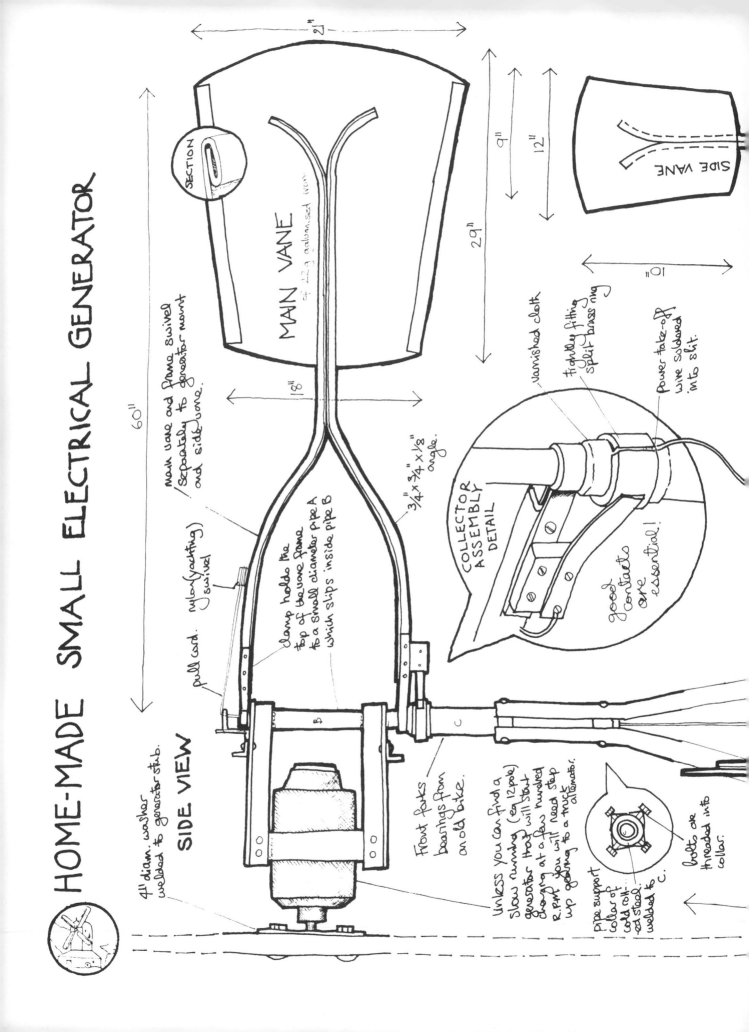

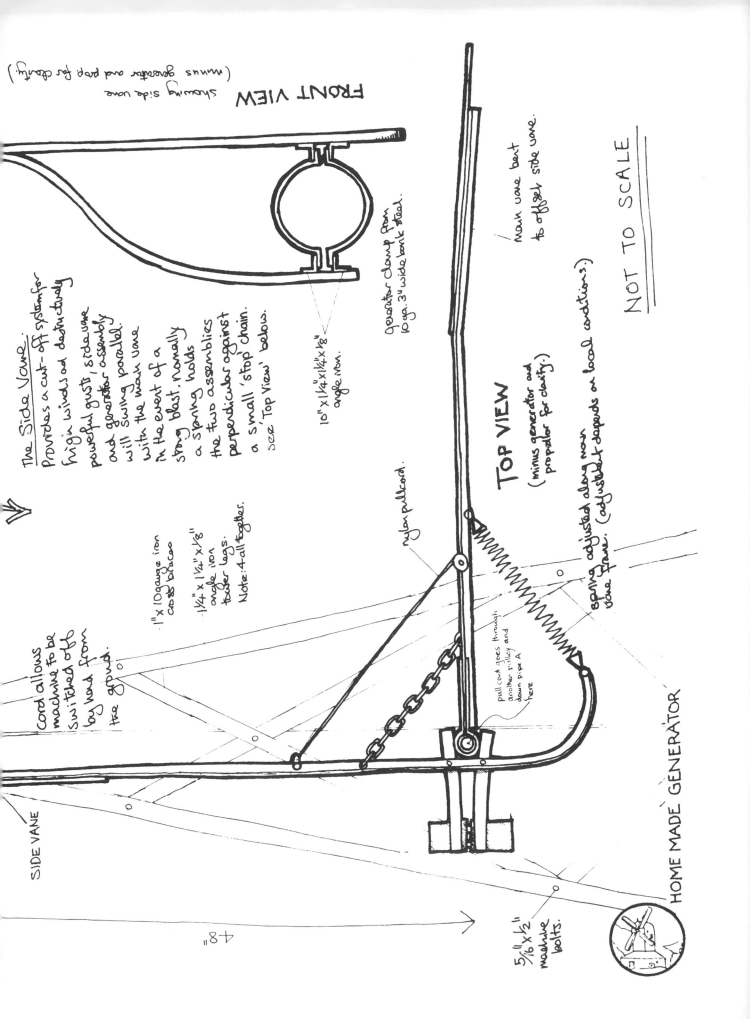

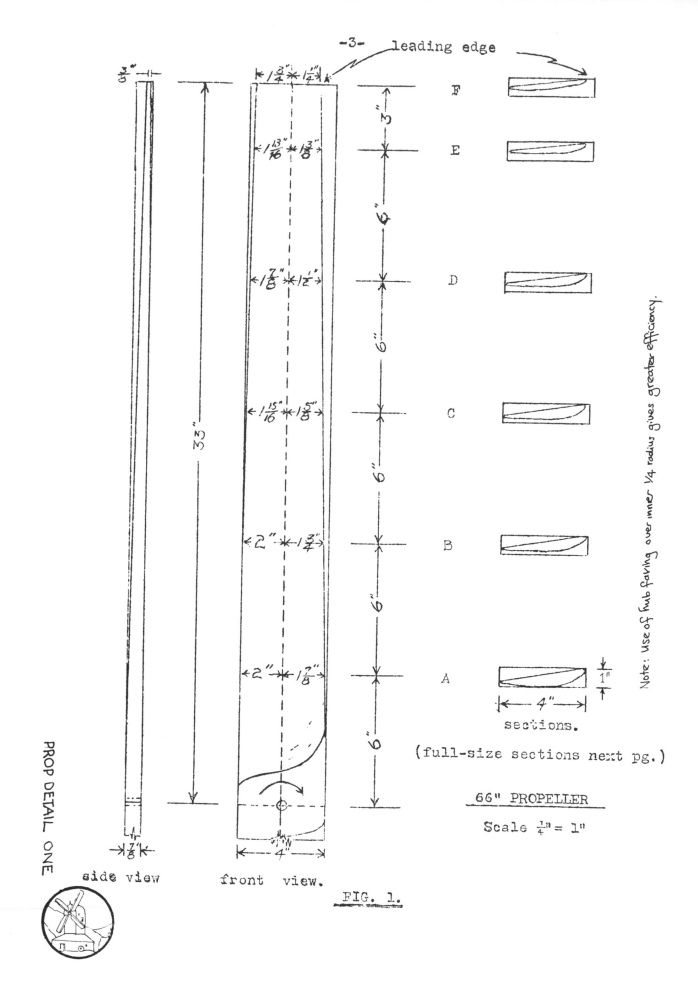

-3- leading edge

F

E

D

C

B

A

sections.

(full-size sections next pg.)

66" PROPELLER

Scale ¼" = 1"

Note: use of hub faring over inner ¼ radius gives greater efficiency.

PROP DETAIL ONE

side view

front view.

FIG. 1.

HOW TO SHAPE THE PROPELLER

WITH THE USE OF PATTERNS'

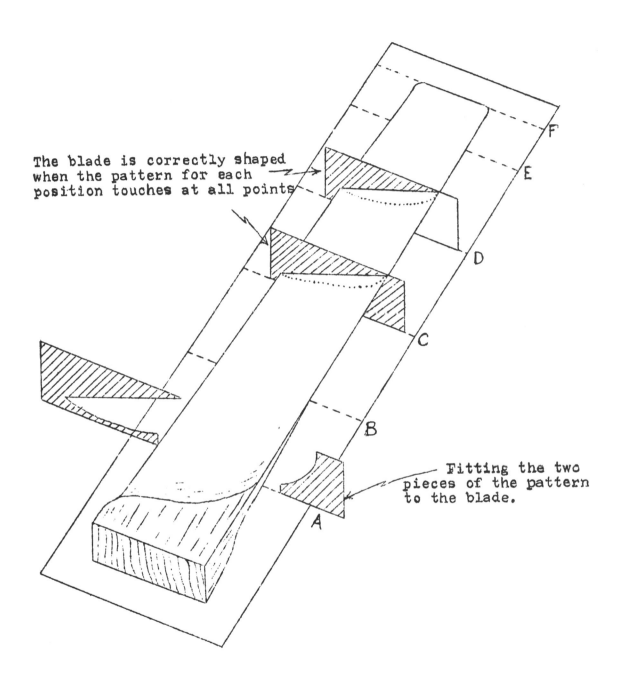

The blade is correctly shaped when the pattern for each position touches at all points

Fitting the two pieces of the pattern to the blade.

FIG. 2

Shape it with a spoke shave or a rasp or a surform.....Best wood? Redwood or straight-grained fir. Willow? Sitka spruce.

PROP DETAIL TWO

FULL SIZE PATTERNS FOR EACH POSITION

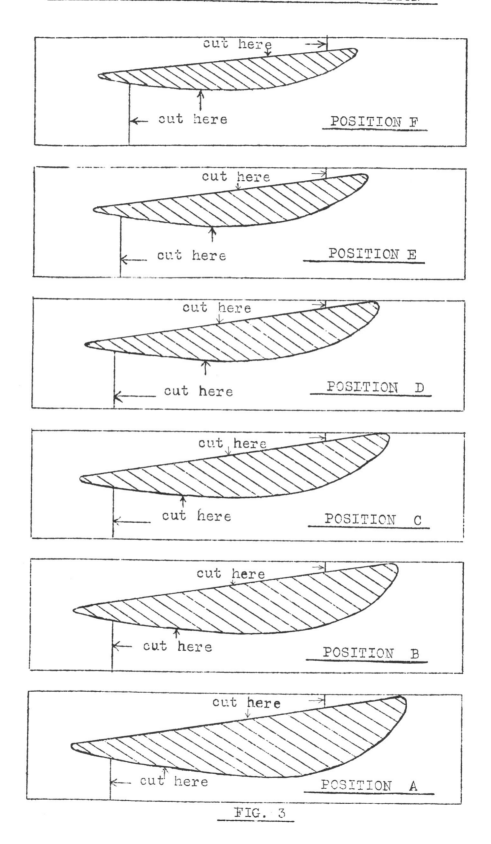

PROP DETAIL 3.

FIG. 3

PROPELLOR FINISHING.

Choice of Wood: Close grain is best to give the prop. rigidity and stiffness. The wood used should be well seasoned and dried out for at least 2 weeks before using. This is important as the blades may lose their balance by uneven drying out.

Balancing the Propellor. A unbalanced propellor will soon destroy itself. Method: place the prop. on a free turning shaft indoors where there are no air currents. The prop. is rotated and allowed to come to rest. The heavier blade will determine the point of rest. A properly balanced prop will come to rest at varying points on repeated testing.

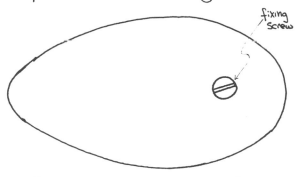

fixing screw

Choose a piece of sheet metal of a weight that would logically balance your propellor. Shape it elliptically and drill an 1/8" hole at the larger end. Now take a 1/2" wood screw and the balancer and hang them from a piece of light thread on the lightest end of the prop. Move the weight along the blade until the prop. is fairly well balanced. Then screw the weight to the blade in that position. Fine adjustment is then made by rotating the shape about the fixing screw. Great care and patience should be taken to thorough balance any propellor. The balance should be re checked at least once a year.

Note: Sealing against moisture must be well done Five coats of enamel or varnish, rubbing down well with wet and dry emery paper between coats is what is needed.

Note: the sophisticated and robust blade feathering mechanism on this old wreck in mid wales.

Two examples of machines that I have recently come across that are going for their scrap value ie. between £10 - 50. Save these old machines good and put them to use.

A Ramshackle HERCULES near Avebury, WILTSHIRE.

PROP FINISH

AUTO-CONTROLS for high

wind gusts that might otherwise endanger the structure.

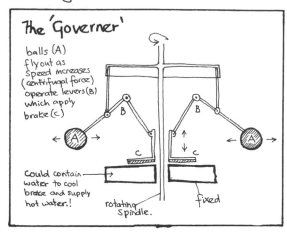

The 'Governer'

balls (A)
fly out as
speed increases
(centrifugal force)
operate levers (B)
which apply
brake (C.)

A → ← A →

Could contain
water to cool
brake and supply
hot water.!

rotating
Spindle.

fixed

PATENTED AIR-BRAKE GOVENOR

Operates by centrifugal force. When wind velocity exceeds 23 miles per hour, governor flaps automatically open and spread wind away from propeller (See illustration). Governor also acts as a fly wheel to maintain even propeller speed and eliminate vibration in gusty wind.

(DYNA TECH. USA.)

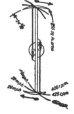

FIG. 65. A homemade Turbine windmill made by attaching rough board fans to the driving wheel and crank of an old reaping machine.
The swivel is the thimble of an old wagon.

THE WIND

"The idea which led to the invention is this; in the ordinary steel mill the fan is struck by the full force of a sudden gust before its mechanism begins to turn it out of the wind and so to adjust it. In the meantime it sustains the shock of the full wind. This led Mr. Baldwin to devise a method whereby the regulating lever should be struck by the blast first, and so throw the fans as to escape the full fury of the wind. He has attained this end in a very clever way. In Fig. 65 may be seen a regulator or rudder-like lever, in front of the fans. The slightest motion of the lever is instantly conveyed to the fans, which are turned edgewise more or less, according to the velocity of the wind, thus adjusting it with nicety."

from. *The Homemade Windmills of Nebraska*

► ITOMATIC GOVERNING DEVICE

SELF GOVERNING

WIND DIRECTION

WINDMILL WORKING POSITION IN LOW AND MEDIUM WINDS.

WIND DIRECTION

WINDMILL WORKING POSITION IN HIGH WINDS. WINDWHEEL TURNS SLIGHTLY OUT OF WIND THUS REGULATING SPEED.

WIND DIRECTION

WINDMILL IN 'OFF' POSITION WITH BRAKE ON, BROUGHT ABOUT BY VIOLENT WINDS OR BY HAND OPERATION OF THE 'PULL IN WINCH.'

The Hercules windmill is designed to work in low windspeeds, as the windspeed increases the automatic governing device comes into action and operates as follows—

The windwheel, due to its position in relation to the centre of the head gear, is

moved slightly at an angle from the direction of the wind by the pressure upon it, this action being assisted by the tail mechanism. As the wind pressure increases so the windwheel is moved further out of the wind, thereby keeping the speed of the windmill within reasonable limits.

During violent storms the windwheel is swung completely out of the wind, the tail assuming a position at right angles to the wheel shaft. As a result, the brake is applied by means of the brake rod and bell crank in the same manner as when the winch is used.

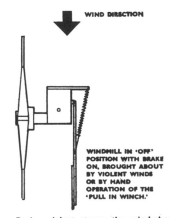

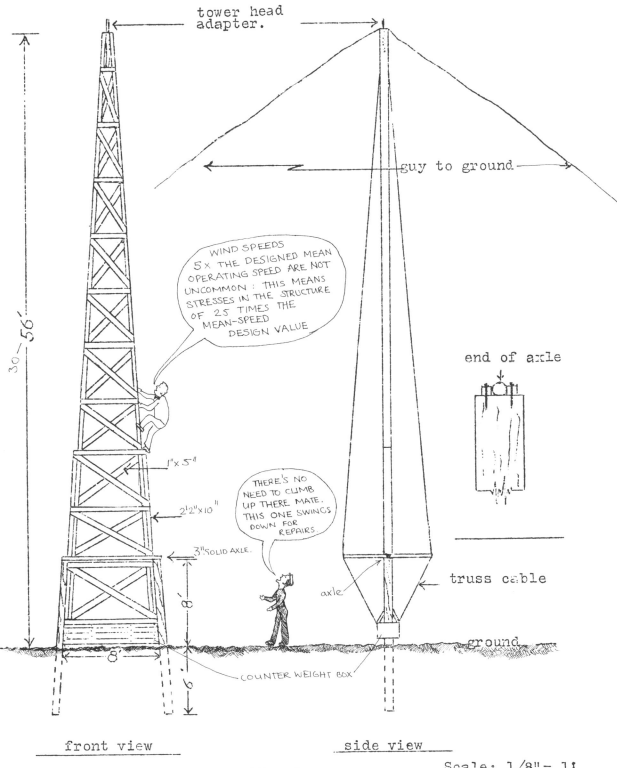

front view   side view

FIG. 5.   Scale: 1/8" = 1'

For Best results locate at least 20 feet above any obstruction within 400 feet.
This is important. Farm buildings such as barns may be used to support windmills; but 6'-10' stub towers do not take the machine out of eddy currents. A
12' tower would be a minimum requirement. It should not be mounted on a house
where the noise of the plant will be transmitted to the living quarters.

POWER TAKE-OFF

Direct power take off from a windmill, such as that illustrated on the right, is a matter of experimenting mechanically with levers, pulleys, cams and so on until you get the sort of motion needed in the right place.

Operating air and water pumps is also fairly straightforward as long as the requirements of the pump and the characteristics of the drive are suitably matched. Constant speeds are often necessary and these may be achieved with governing devices or by absorbing short term variations of drive within a flywheel. (often a pump will have an inate capacity for governing drive speed.

Electrical generation is the most ubiquitous use to which a mill can be put but needs care as electrical generating equipment does not usually have a wide operating tolerance.

Most auto type generators will need either a step up gearing (1:3 — 1:10.) or modification to run at slow speeds. They are normally made to run at between 1,500 rpm and 3,500 rpm and cut-in (i.e. start charging.) at 650 rpm slowest, whilst the high speed aerofoil windmill will rarely exceed 1000 r.p.m. If gearing is used it must be precision made as great losses of efficiency may occur with crude belt drives etc.

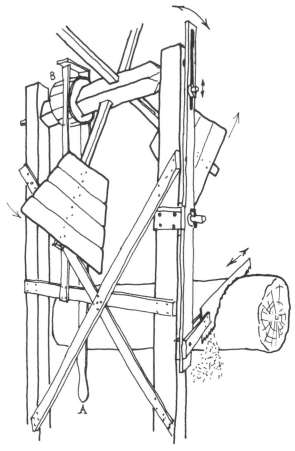

The Battle-ax windmill of Mr A.G. Tingley, Verdon, Nebraska sawing a thirty-inch log. Diameter of wheel ten feet.

✳ In an age when working hours are not fixed or imposed by economic interdependence and social exploitation the rythmn of peoples utilisation of energy can adapt itself to the caprices of supply, so people work closely with ever changing natural elements.

✳ The Sturmey Archer bicycle Dynohub sold by Raliegh will provide its rated output (low.) with the addition of 2ft. diameter blades and without any modification ✳ Bike parts are generally useful in windmill construction) This type will keep a small auto battery charged up so a small electric light and a radio may be powered.

✳ Electricity travels badly at low voltages (due to heat losses.) and a transformer for domestic quantities of electricity (1+kw) is costly, so things are best kept close together.

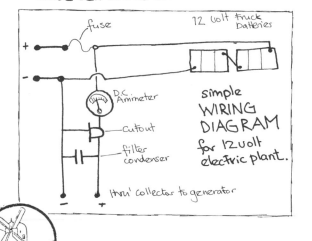

fuse

12 volt truck batteries

D.C. Ammeter

Cutout

filter condenser

thru' collector to generator

simple
WIRING
DIAGRAM
for 12 volt
electric plant.

TAKE OFF

GLASS-REINFORCED-POLYESTER (resin) PROPELLOR

Paper honeycomb 'hexel' is coated with fibreglass or G.R.P. (glass reinforced poly-ester resin) to give an extremely strong and lightweight hollow structure. First the hexel is cut to the required shape with a saw whilst in a compressed state. It is then stretched out to the correct length with an aluminium rod through the centre of the blade. (see below.)

The hexel is then given a strong cladding of several layers of G.R.P. The fibreglass technique allows you to have an extremely sharp trailing edge. For even more strength the fibreglass itself may be reinforced will stainless steel fibres etc.
P.S. It might be worth trying an aerofoil or circular section fibreglass tower. (cf. recent yacht masts. aluminum 12" diam.)

Stretching a piece of hexcel which will be fiberglassed and made into a windmill blade.

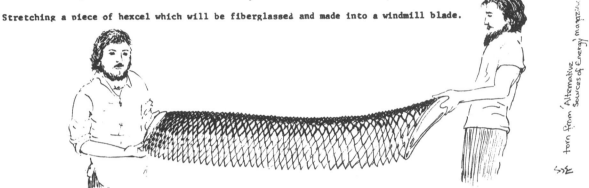

torn from 'Alternative Sources of Energy' magazine.

SERIOUSLY THO'

When you get confident and want to make the big one that will give you bountiful heaps of energy so that you can leave the lights on all night etc . . . .

The BRACE research institute of Quebec made a nice job using 3 blade (speed and stability.) propellors* fixed pitch (aerofoil section NACA 4415.) These are mounted (downwind orientation) onto an Austin 5 ton truck rear axle. The differential is locked and the 7.2 : 1 gearing trans-mitts power down to a pump (which also limits props speeds in winds of over 30 mph.) The mast is made from rectangular hollow section steel and the whole of the central mast rotates using truck parts. Auto. parts are used again (clutch + 8 speed gearbox.) between the drive and pump to gain the best performance at all wind speeds.

This prototype, tested in Barbados in the late '60s, attained 30 horse power at speeds of 30 mph! At 10 mph. (British Average.) it was still producing a hearty one horse power. However the prop. diam. was 32ft., not a size for the beginner.

* G.R.P.

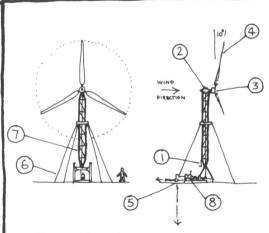

WIND DIRECTION

10'

① HAND CRANK TO GET IT GOING IN LOW SPEEDS

② 5 TON AUSTIN AXLE

③ TRUCK WHEEL HUB (HAND BRAKE STILL ATTACHED.)

④ GLASS FIBRE / EPOXY RESIN AEROFOILS.

⑤ WATER PUMP

⑥ GUYS TO MONOLITHIC REINFORCED CONCRETE FOUNDATION.

⑦ TOWER 30 FEET HIGH.

⑧ 8 SPEED LANDROVER GEARBOX.

FURTHER

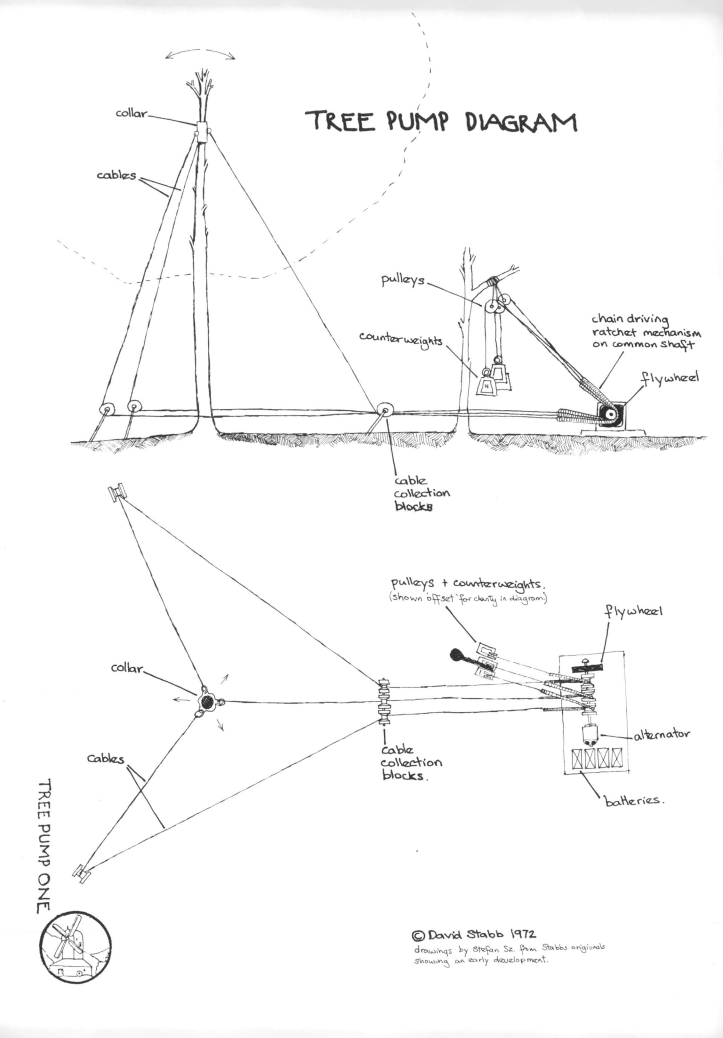

TREE PUMP DIAGRAM

collar

cables

pulleys

counterweights

chain driving ratchet mechanism on common shaft

flywheel

cable collection blocks

pulleys + counterweights.
(shown 'offset' for clarity in diagram.)

flywheel

collar

cable collection blocks.

cables

alternator

batteries.

TREE PUMP ONE

© David Stabb 1972

drawings by Stefan Sz. from Stabbs originals
showing an early development.

Fig 4

TREE PUMP 2.

THE MOVEMENTS OF A TREE IN THE WIND ARE TRANSFERRED TO ROTARY MECHANICAL POWER BY THE METHOD INDICATED. THE PURPOSE OF THIS METHOD IS TO MAKE AVAILABLE FOR HARNASSING MUCH LARGER 'SWEPT AREAS' OF WIND THAN COULD BE NORMALLY EXPECTED FROM DOMESTIC SCALE WIND MACHINES. SIMPLY BY VIRTUE OF ITS SIZE AND HEIGHT A LARGISH TREE HAS A GOOD DEAL OF POWER WHICH IT CAN SPARE AND WHEN IT DOES MOVE THERE REALLY IS SOME FORCE.

A TREE IS A READY MADE ENERGY SYSTEM INTO WHICH MAN CAN PARTICIPATE — WITHIN REASON. TREES ARE DESIGNED FOR THE WORST STORM CONDITIONS AND CONSEQUENTLY TEND TO BE OVER-STRUCTURED FOR AVERAGE CONDITIONS. IT IS THIS PORTION OF THE TREE'S ENERGY WHICH MAN IS INVITED TO JOIN.

David Stabb. 1972.

Note: SMALL DISTANCE LARGE FORCES CAN EASILY BE SPREAD OUT BY THE USE OF PULLEYS. (AS WITH SMALL HOISTS — BUT IN REVERSE)

TREE PUMP 2

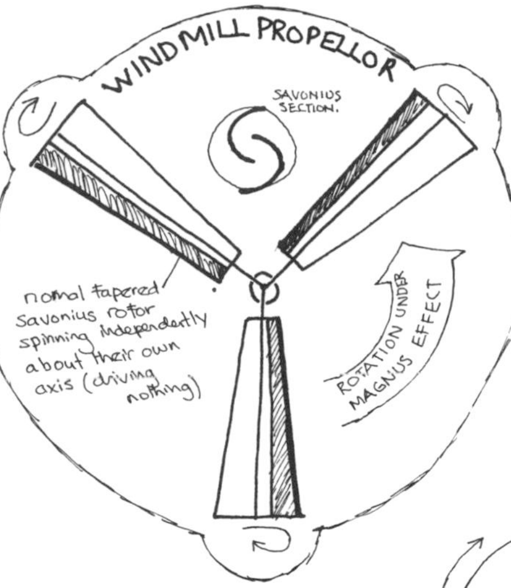

WINDMILL PROPELLOR

SAVONIUS SECTION.

normal tapered savonius rotor spinning independantly about their own axis (driving nothing)

ROTATION UNDER MAGNUS EFFECT

VARIATIONS OF ALL KINDS ARE POSSIBLE ON THIS THEME. THE IDEA IS TO GET THE HIGHEST + LARGEST SWEPT AREA USING SIMPLE MAT- -ERIALS + CONSTRUCTION AND A REASONABLE EFFICIENCY OF OPERATION.

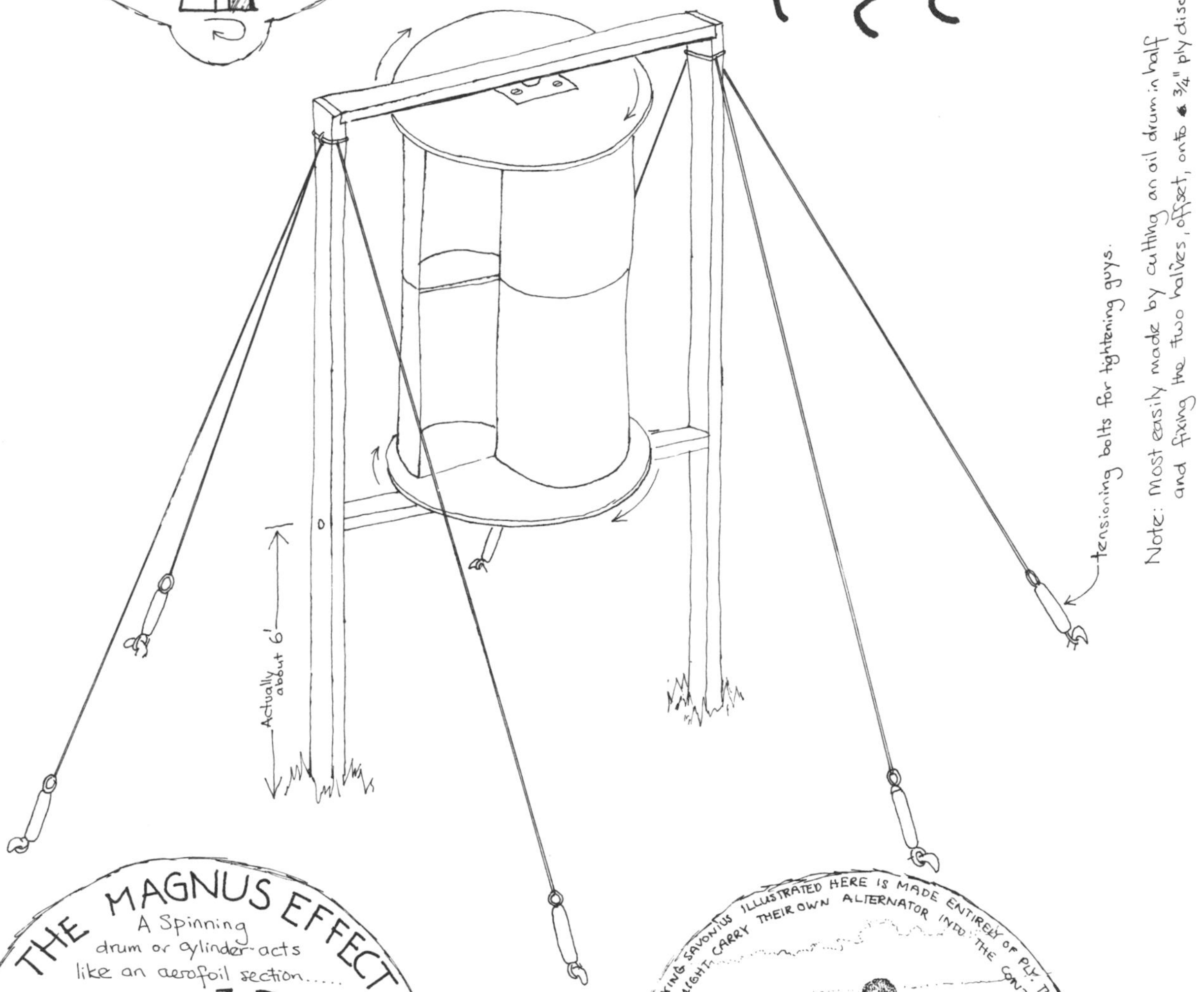

Note: Most easily made by cutting an oil drum in half and fixing the two halves, offset, onto ¾" ply discs.

tensioning bolts for tightening guys.

Actually about 6'

SAVONIUS

THE MAGNUS EFFECT

A spinning drum or cylinder acts like an aerofoil section......

WIND

↑lift.

The lift is equivalent to an aerofoil of perfect section 4× the diameter of the cylinder. Anton Flefnor sailed a big boat across the Atlantic in the 30's using this principle; Driving cylinders with a small engine. Savonius rotors will fly like a kite or glider using this effect.

May also be used to make windmill propellor. see right → + above.

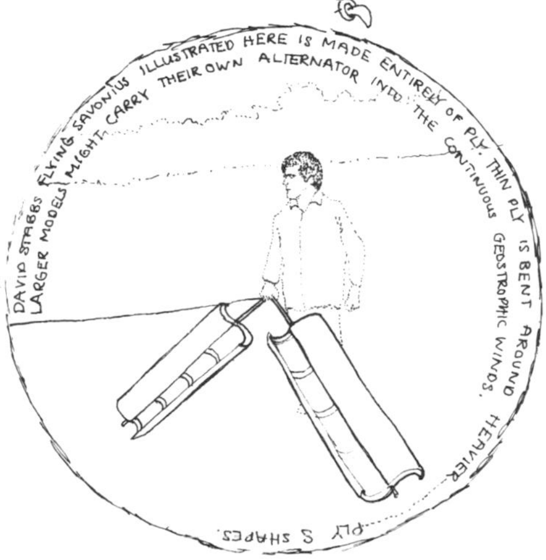

DAVID STRABES FLYING SAVONIUS ILLUSTRATED HERE IS MADE ENTIRELY OF PLY. THIN PLY LARGER MODELS MIGHT CARRY THEIR OWN ALTERNATOR INTO THE CONTINUOUS GEOSTROPHIC WINDS.

IS BENT AROUND HEAVIER

PLY S SHAPES.

FIRE

In a survival situation fire is as important pyschologically as it is for warmth and cooking.

There are three parts to the process of making a fire each of which may be varied in several ways.

    i. The spark or starting light.
    ii. The tinder.
    iii. Fuel of varying grades.

The Spark:

    a. sunlight focused by a glass, any convex shaped transparent object may be tried although a more certain result is assured if the glass is optically made (as found in telescope or other optical instrument.) Remarkable though it sounds burning glasses have been shaped from ice. Highly polished concave surfaces may sometimes be able to focus the necessary energy.
note: When focusing sun rays to start a fire try to use black tinder.

    b. Flint struck against hard steel will produce sparks. The flint may be replaced by any silaceous stone such as agate, rock crystal or quartz (also broken crockery.) Any Blacksmith can make a good steel from an old file.

    c. Matches. The main trouble with Lucifers comes from wind putting them out. Throw a cloak or blanket over your head whilst you operate and have an abundance of small twigs. Another method of lighting a match in a breeze is to make a cone from paper. Turning its apex into the wind you strike the match into the cone. The paper will soon burn with a flame too strong to be snuffed out by a single blast of air.

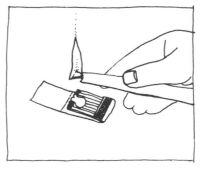

This is how to make matches waterproof.

When there is nothing dry to strike the match against scratch its head with the edge of a knife or finger nail. It is well to carry one or two water--proof match cases and/or some wax sealed matches if you are a traveller.

    d. Fire sticks. Rubbing 2 sticks together to cause a fire is a difficult and skilled task but one that is used by most primitive people. A drill--stick is rotated against a fixed 'fire-block'. The drill stick may be any tough, hard and dry stick but the block must be of little grain, mediumly soft, and readily immflamable. Ivy is best. Walnut is also reasonable. Francis Galton in 'The Art of Travel' reckons that it is fairly easy to produce smoke but 3 men would need a couple of hours practice to produce fire. once you've got the knack it takes between 1 and 3 minutes to produce fire. Keep trying for periods no longer than 4 minutes with rests in between.

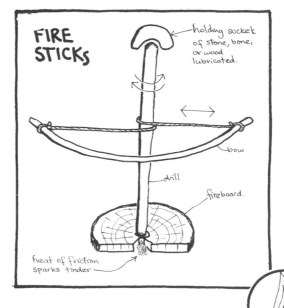

FIRE STICKS

holding socket of stone, bone, or wood lubricated.

bow

drill

fireboard.

heat of friction sparks tinder

SPARK

FIRE : TINDER.

There are two main types of tinder, those that need a box in which to keep them and those less friable that can be grasped.

a. Tinders needing a box. Rags, dry dung, dry moss, birch and cedar bark, lichen; also, but not as good, grass, dead evergreen needles and pulverised dry rotten wood. Tinder boxes are often simply a hollow cylinder of wood or metal about 3 inches long and corked at one end. Rags lighted and then put out before they reach white ash, are best. This kind of tinder is often made in the box in which it is to be kept or by dowsing a flaming rag with sand.

b. Tinders not needing a box. A roll of rag, cotton lampwick, roll of touch paper, hair from certain plants, a long string of pith sewn up in a sheath, amadou (made from fungi and saltpetre.)
Cotton rag will take fire from a flint spark only in very dry conditions. It must be rolled up tight leaving the end of the roll 'fluffy.' 'Touch-paper' is unsized paper dipped in a solution of saltpetre. In all cases the addition of saltpetre to tinder will make it burn better. It exists in the ashes of many plants such as tobacco, dill, maize and sunflower.

FUEL.

As Francis Galton points out, there is a knack in finding good firewood (I never have quite got it myself.) but the only suggestions he makes are to look under bushes and to pull roots from rotten stumps.
Care must be taken that dead wood in hedges is not collected where it could be there to fill some weak spot.

<u>Types of Wood</u> : Weight of wood is a good indication of its heating value.
Best woods are; —
Hickory, Beech, Oak, Ash (burns green) Apple (sweet smelling.) Birch, Elm, Lime (v. dry.) Holley (gives good embers) Hawthorn (little smoke.) Sycamore (dry)

2nd choices are; —
Chestnut (better if seasoned) Elder, (bitter smoke) maple (dry). Softwoods are good for kindling but do not give sustained heat.
The dead and fallen timber from one acre of fairly intensive woodland will give about 150 cu.ft. of firewood per year. If you have waste land that is too poor or steep for crops why not grow trees. Although trees take many years to mature they prevent soil erosion, <u>make</u> soil, act as shelter-belts and can provide a useful crop.

<u>Peat</u> burns gently with a sweet smell and a warm glow. It is cut in turves a foot or two below the surface during summer, stacked edgeways to dry and turned regularly until drying is complete. This takes 10-12 days. It is then carted home and piled under cover or made into a rick and thatched for winter use.
Heating value is about ½ that of coal (per unit weight.) but it makes less dirt and has a pleasant fragrance. Bellows are handy to put new life into the fire if it should dwindle unexpectedly.

Other minor fuels are dried cow dung, bones and seaweed, of use if wood is not available.

OUTDOOR FIRES

A popular fire structure is the star shape, with large logs, their ends within a fire of smaller pieces. As they are burnt they are pushed inward.

Another good pattern is parallel logs with the burning end facing the wind. In this way the logs gradually burn along their length. A 'green' log at the end of this fire will make it smoulder right through the night.

✳ The use of 'reflective' surfaces to direct heat where it is wanted (eg. into a tent.) are worthwhile and may be simply made from logs.

✳ For the main fuel a large log is always worth more than many small logs.

✳ Wet-Weather Firemaking: Arrangements of Birch bark are best if it is available. Small dead evergreen twigs bunched in the hand are also good. Another device is the fuzz-stick, which is a shaven stick with a mass of the shavings left attached. In very wet conditions dry kindling that will burn from a match or tinder may only be available by splitting logs and getting splinters from the inside. A rotten pine log or stump will provide resinous branch stumps that will burn strongly.

Several small fires give more usable heat than one huge one.

"The Ovampos, as they travel, collect sticks, each man his own faggot, and when they stop, each collects eight or nine stones as large as bricks and larger and sets them up in a circle; and within these he lights up his little fire. Now the party make their fireplaces close together, in two or more parallel lines, and sleep in between them; the stones prevent the embers from flying about and doing mischief, and also, after the fires have quite burnt out, they continue to radiate heat."

reported by Francis Galton in The Art of Travel.

✳ A small conical shape fire is a good structure for quick heat. A method of doing this is to push 3 soft wood sticks into the ground with their tops touching; other sticks may then be built around with smaller material inside.

Living in a town logs are more difficult to come by. If you live in a place without a lot of scrap lumber you can substitute newspapers rolled up tight until about 6" thick. The newspaper is kept rolled with a bit of wire or by rolling on the diagonal in another paper and tucking the ends in.

from Whole Earth Cat.

Safety Pointers.

✳ never leave an open fire unguarded.

✳ Do not make a fire where it could spread to the surrounding vegetation. It is best to clear all grass etc from the immediate surrounds of the fire.

✳ Quench all fire with earth or water before leaving it.

P.S. The secret of success in firemaking is in very gradually increasing the size of fuel in 5 or 6 stages through; — tinder, matchsize, pencil, little finger, forefinger, stakes and finally logs, making sure each stage is well caught before adding the next

CAMP

COOKING FIRES

Hay box Cooking : I thought this meant a big pile of green hay which actually built up enough heat (from its own de--composition.) to cook something, but the only operating details that I have found concerning hayboxes use the straw as a super insulant. Dishes such as stews, soups, porridge or prunes, are brought to the boil and then placed in a biscuit tin or something similar that is insulated with as much straw as possible. Mrs. Beeton recommends a box 30"x 24" x 24" lined with newspaper and stuffed with hay. The cooking vessel is covered with a flannel (over the normal lid.) and cooked for about four times as long as it would be if cooked normally. Useful if you are without an oven or short of fuel.

Another method that relies on keeping in the heat is to dig a hole about 2' deep and light a fire at the bottom. Stones are then placed on the fire and covered with green leaves. Food is placed on these leaves and covered with more leaves. The hole is then filled with earth. Dig up dinner later. Good if you are going out to do some work and want a hot meal ready when you come back.

Embers are particularly useful for delicate gourmet camp cooking as they give off a steady heat. The 'keyhole' type cooking fire has a main blaze in a circular hole and a shallow trench cut away to one side of this hole into which the embers are raked and above which the tasty kebab (or whatever you fancy) is cooked. Small animals may be baked <u>in</u> the embers of a fire if covered in clay mud. Fish may also be cooked in this way wrapped in leaves and then covered in clay.

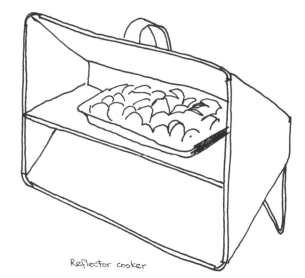

Reflector cooker

Cast Iron 'Dutch Oven'

STOVES

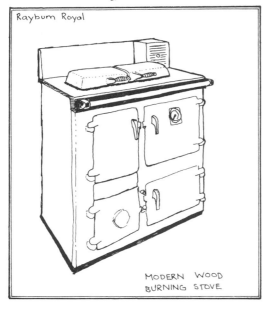

Rayburn Royal
MODERN WOOD BURNING STOVE

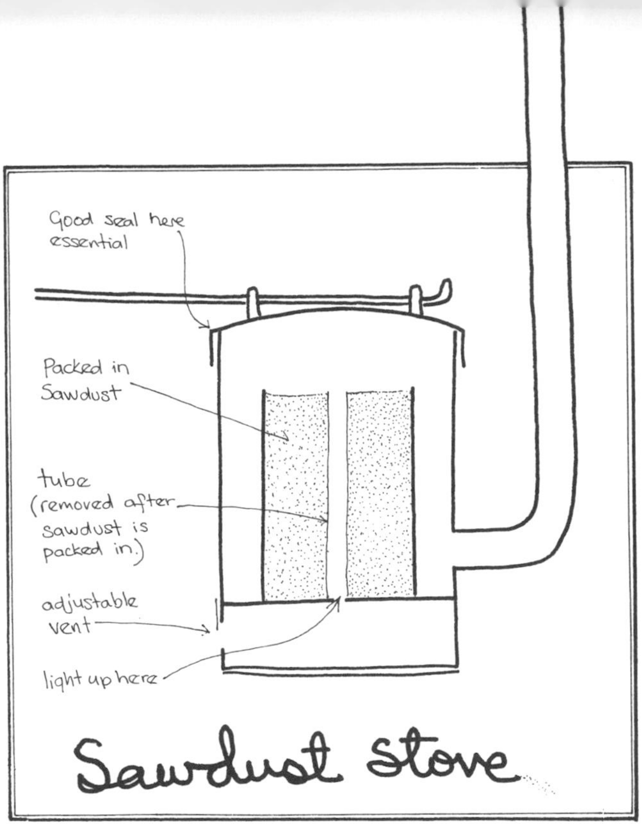

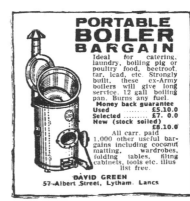

Good seal here essential
Packed in Sawdust
tube (removed after sawdust is packed in.)
adjustable vent
light up here
Sawdust Stove

A fire enclosed within a simple fire-proof box becomes safer and more easily controlled. As the box becomes more sophisticated provision is made for hot plates, oven, hot water and ducted warm air.
One of the most flexible of these multi-use stoves is the 'Rayburn', shown above which burns wood or a number of solid fuels. It cooks and provides hot water. cost £ 130 new £ 10–50 s/h.

PORTABLE
BOILER
BARGAIN
Ideal for catering, laundry, boiling pig or poultry food, beetroot, tar, lead, etc. Strongly built, these ex-Army boilers will give long service. 12 gall boiling pan. Burns any fuel.
Money back guarantee
Used £5.10.0
Selected £7. 0.0
New (stock soiled) £8.10.0
All carr. paid
1,000 other useful bargains including coconut matting, wardrobes, folding tables, filing cabinets, tools etc. illus list free.
DAVID GREEN
57 Albert Street, Lytham. Lancs

N.B. A stove is twice as efficient as an open fire.

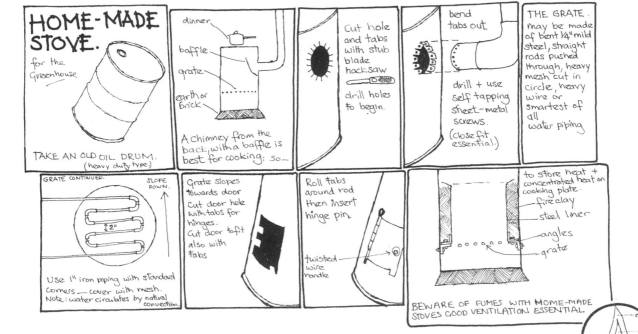

HOME-MADE STOVE.
for the Greenhouse
TAKE AN OLD OIL DRUM. (heavy duty type.)
dinner
baffle
grate
earth or brick
A chimney from the back, with a baffle is best for cooking: so—
Cut hole and tabs with stub blade hacksaw
drill holes to begin.
bend tabs out
drill + use self tapping sheet-metal screws.
(close fit essential.)
THE GRATE.
may be made of bent 1/4" mild steel, straight rods pushed through, heavy mesh cut in circle, heavy wire or smartest of all water piping
GRATE CONTINUED.
SLOPE DOWN.
2"
Use 1" iron piping with standard corners — cover with mesh.
Note: water circulates by natural convection.
Grate slopes towards door
Cut door hole with tabs for hinges.
Cut door to fit also with tabs
Roll tabs around rod then insert hinge pin
twisted wire handle
to store heat + concentrated heat on cooking plate.
fireclay
steel liner
angles
grate
BEWARE OF FUMES WITH HOME-MADE STOVES GOOD VENTILATION ESSENTIAL

c
b
a

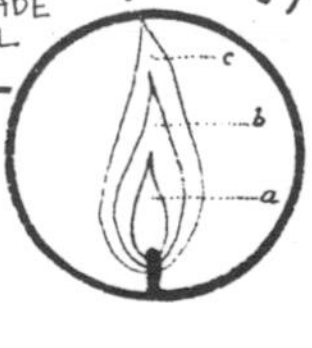

FIREPLACE.

The sensation of comfort that is engendered in most of us by the living rooms of many old houses centres around the design of the fireplace and inglenooks. These artefacts are embued with more meaning than may be simply associated with their heating function. The most efficient heater is a well designed enclosed stove —— fireplaces are generally less than 25% efficient, most of the heat going up the chimney (ie. only ¼ of the heat content of the fuel is given out to the room.) nevertheless the mysterious qualities of the open hearth are lost in most 'modern' heating devices. These qualities, that make a considerable difference to the living environ, need not necessarily be lost in improving heating efficiency.

To get the most from your flames check your hearth for the following 'good design features';——

FLUE IS BEST 7" diameter ROUND SECTION (2nd best rectangular 9" X 12".)

CHIMNEY STACK LOCATED AWAY FROM OUTSIDE WALL IF POSSIBLE, to reduce heat losses and keep smoke temperature steady.

1" ROCKWOOL INSULATION to reduce temperature differential up chimney (and ∴ improve draft.)

RESTRICTED NECK induces venturi effect (increase in speed) combats downdraft.

AIR HEATED AT BACK OF FIRE CONVECTS AROUND THE ROOM SPREADING WARMTH.

5"

SMOKESHELF reduces backdraft and smoking danger

CORRECTLY SHAPED NARROWED CHIMNEY THROAT WITH NO JUTTING IRREGULARITIES AVOID SMOKING.

HOT AIR

SAFETY COVER FOR OVERNIGHT SLOW BURNING

4"

WATER PIPES heat up.

7"

INCLINED FIRE BACK retains higher grate temperature (could be more angled than shown)

NOTE: COMBUSTION AIR DRAFT IS PROVIDED THROUGH A SEPARATE DUCT FROM OUTSIDE OR VENTILATED LOBBY TO SIDE OF HEARTH. THIS AVOIDS DRAFTS IN ROOM AND, WITH THE 'HOT BOX' BEHIND THE FIRE, PROVIDES A CONTROLLED WARMED AIR VENTILATION SYSTEM.

SHALLOW GRATE

ASH CAN

BACK DIMENSION SHOULD ≃ DEPTH OF RECESS. (Count Rumfords Rule of Thumb.)

OiL

Limited supplies running out fast. And until it does Agro-Kemikal Kapitalism produces every ounce of profit/pollution it can manage. Being realistic things won't change by quiet avoidance (the most ardent ecofreaks ride on the internal combustion engine now and again.) Briefly discussed here are some fossil fueled devices that are immediately useful on account of their mobility or other characteristics that make them worth having around in situations such as squatting or living nomadically. They are often of a type of mechanism that could convert to other renewable oil sources such as those squeezed out of vegetable seeds (Rape cabbage, linseed, sunflower, olive, castor....) and to other 'renewable' fuels such as alcohol from distillation (see section on alcohol.)

Candles: Played an important part in lighting where a local source of oil had not been found. Candles were made from mutton fat (or tallow) melted down and poured into moulds around the wick.

Oil Lamps: These were originally crude affairs being pottery bowls with wicks of twisted moss prot--ruding from a spout.

Moorish Lamp found at the Mines of Gar-Rouban, in Algeria.

L'A Fauvel

EMERGENCY TIN CAN LAMP
(paraffin or) oil soaked cotton wool
lighter wick or cotton string

To make a quick version of the primitive lamp in emergencies, take a saucer. Put a length of thick cotton string into the saucer. Leave one end slightly above the rim. Pour some cooking fat (dripping or oil) into the saucer.

Light the emergent end. (Be careful not to set the fat alight.)

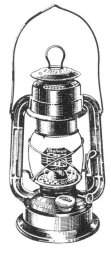

*The first important improvement was introduced in France by Meunier in 1780, when a burner was designed having a flat band or ribbon wick and a metallic chimney; but the most valuable improvement was that introduced by ARGAND of Geneva, which was patented in England in 1783. In this form of lamp a cylindrical wick was used, placed between two metal tubes, through the inner of which a current of air was allowed to pass to the inside of the flame, in addition to that which was maintained round its outer circumference by means of a chimney, at first of metal, placed some distance above the wick, but soon after constructed of glass. This lamp afforded a white and brilliant light of much greater power than any that had been previously available, and its discovery was hailed as affording the means of pursuing many delicate kinds of work which previously had been restricted to daylight.

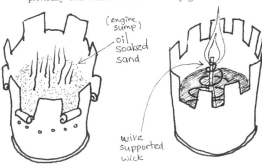

(engine sump) oil soaked sand

wire supported wick

TIN CAN COOKERS

FOSSIL POWER

PARAFFIN IS THE CHEAPEST
AVAILABLE OIL FUEL FOR
HEATERS AND LAMPS.
PARAFFIN GIVES ABOUT 9000 B.Th.U.
PER GALLON. SEA GAS costs
half as much again for the same
heat whilst electricity cost 2½
times as much.

Radiant Heater
Model R1A

R1A with
Light Conversion
Head CHI fitted

Self-Priming Storm Lantern Model BR49B

A specially developed version of the Tilley Stormlight. The lantern can be lit using kerosene/paraffin from the container of the lamp. Originally made for British Railways, this lamp is now in use by many concerns and individuals who find it convenient to eliminate the need for torch and methylated spirit container.

Made in Northern Ireland by Tilley Lamp Co. Dunmurray, Belfast.

TILLEY LAMPS

These pressure kerosene burners
are the best generally available.
The R1A, shown above, gives 1¼ Kwh.
of heat and 1½ pints of paraffin
will give 12 hours burning time.
The light conversion head gives
2000 mean reflected candle power
which is much brighter than most
domestic electric lights.

Floodlight
Projector
Model FL6

5000 mean reflected candle power.

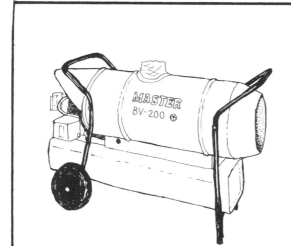

This heater gives out tremendous
heat from a small unit by forced air
ventilation of a paraffin burner.
Good and cheap as a space
heater for halls, domes, marquees etc.
Continuous operation for 13-17 hours
Odourless combustion.
Switch on starting.
Thermostatically controlled.
Cost only 3p per hour to run (14½ kw.
model.)
14½ - 94 kw models available

Made in U.S.A.
British Distributor : W.C. Youngman Ltd.
Industrial Sales Division
Manor Royal, Crawley, SUSSEX.

ESSO BLUE

GASₛₛ..

Calor gas is propane. A gas obtained from the refining of crude oil. It is a 'clean' gas with almost no sulphur or poisonous content. The liquid gas in cylinders is a very mobile source of energy and if you can accomodate the larger sized cylinders then it is only a little more expensive than piped natural gas. Calor gas is to be recommended over other 'makes' on account of its flexibility of use with a wide range of appliances and its numerous suppliers.

A book listing all current U.K. suppliers may be obtained from Calor gas H.Q.

SAFETY PRECAUTIONS

1. Cylinders should be stored vertical. Cylinder housings should be well ventilated and fire proofed.

2. Use the proper flexible tubes, nozzles and connectors. Ask your local dealer for advice.

3. Calor gas has a distinctive smell which gives warning of gas escape and allows leaks to be traced.

4. When fitting a new cylinder make sure all taps are off before opening the full cylinder value.

5. The danger of inadequate ventilation cannot be overemphasised.

APPLIANCE	VENTILATION
Portable fire	6 sq. ins.
2 burner cooker	13 sq. ins.
griller hot plate	25 sq. ins.
small oven	35 sq. ins
water heater	40 sq. ins.

CALOR GAS publish a card detailing safety precautions for the inside of your cupboard door.

Bullfinch Handilight
Portable lantern with all-round flood of brilliant light. Ruby or amber glasses extra. Enamel reflector extra.

Tilley 820 Site Light
Portable inspection lamp, also site huts, etc., where more elaborate arrangements are not possible.

STREAMLITE LAMP
Puts a light on the job inside or out—runs for 30 hours on one gas fill.

Tilley BT25G Floodlight
13" chromed copper parabolic reflector with armour-plate glass. Shock resistant mantle. Sturdy all-weather galvanised finish. 10,000 c.p. beam. Runs off propane or butane.

Fitted to a 10½ lb cylinder of BOC propane, this will give brilliant light for 40 hours.

Bullfinch 'mini-flood'

Bullfinch Auto-Flood
High intensity floodlight with automatic ignition. Also for gantry mounting. 1595 manual ignition model available. Both with 10,000 c.p. beam.

Bullfinch Multi-light Mast
Each binary lens gives a high intensity light beam of over 20,000 c.p.

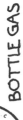

BOTTLE GAS

1225 Boiling Ring
Primarily designed for wash boilers. Also suitable for heating tea urns and pans. For low pressure operation.

D3 Boiling Ring
Simple boiling ring ideal for water boiling in site huts, etc. For low pressure operation.

Double Burner Unit
A high pressure unit for site hut use. Can be used outdoors.

DIXIE TWO STOVE

MAIN MINOR 'B'
An extremely compact instantaneous water heater. Can be connected to water main or storage tank—ideal for houses and caravans. Height 14⅞ (inc. spout) width 13¼", depth 6¼".

DEAN 922
Galvanised casing and brass tap. Readily takes normal-sized wash. Height 29½", width 22", depth 23½".

Savoy Griller 27E
Heavy duty, big capacity griller. Cooks minute steaks in under a minute. Or 540 pieces of toast per hour. 3 separately controlled burners. Solid top heats container foods.

GAS APPLIANCES

SUPER SER CATALYTIC F12 HEATER

Parkinson Cowan portable heater Series FB 1
The heater fits directly onto a 10½ lb BOC propane cylinder, which provides continuous heat for 30 hours. The FB 1 heater is hand-portable and can be used for local heating, such as thawing or drying, or for heating diesel vehicles. It can easily be carried with one hand.

LMD 350

Double Ceramic Plac,
(Single plac model also available) High output radiant heater for workshops, warehouses, etc. New trolley platform increases mobility — eases cylinder changes.
Input (double plac): 25,000 Btu/hr.
(single plac): 12,500 Btu/hr.

PORTABLE GAS FIRE
The gas fire you can pick up and put down wherever you need that extra warmth.

BUTAIRE 22

PORTABLE GAS POKER
No more messing with paper—Calor Poker lights a fire for about 2d.

BIO-GAS 1

METHANE GAS FROM THE BACTERIALOGICAL DECOMPOSITION OF EXCRETA AND OTHER ORGANIC 'WASTES' OR RESIDUES.

✳ In 1952 there were over 1000 working installations producing regular free gas. Today in India there are well over 2,500. ✓

✳ It seems to be fairly simple to cook up some horse dung and straw in an old boiler (at 75°–95°F approx.) full of water and produce gas which will power a bunsen burner. (see right.) However this simple apparatus is rather impractical for processing regular loadings of waste to produce a domestic gas supply.

✳ Every precaution should be taken to avoid getting a mixture of air and methane as a 5–14% methane in air mixture is EXPLOSIVE. All junctions should be carefully tested and naked flames avoided near gas holders. N.B. A pressure build up over 98 lbs. sq. in will explode if air is present.

✳ Generally speaking 1 lb weight of fresh cow-dung will produce one cubic foot of gas at 75°F. With more sophisticated temperature controls up to 1.5 cu.ft. may be obtained. A cow or horse will give from 10–16 metric tons of dung per year. To this may be added an equal quantity of vegetable matter.

✳ Horse, pig and chicken dung are worth more, in gas terms, than cow dung. Vegetable waste, which may make up 50% of the mix by volume, gives about 7 cu.ft of gas for each pound _dry_ weight. Humans excrete only a meagre 5 ounces of turd per day so to get a useful amount of gas per person participant you must suppliment human donations with animal dung and vegetable wastes. Note: Human excreta is worth adding as it enriches the residue which is used as compost.

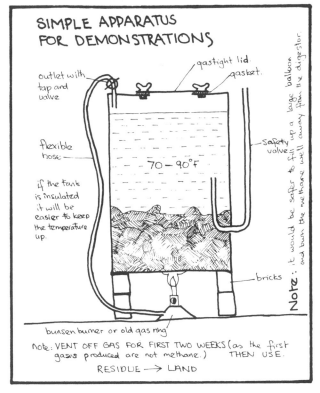

SIMPLE APPARATUS FOR DEMONSTRATIONS

outlet with tap and valve — gastight lid. — gasket.

flexible hose —

70 – 90°F

if the tank is insulated it will be easier to keep the temperature up.

safety valve —

— bricks

Note: it would be safer to fill up a large balloon and burn the methane well away from the digester.

bunsen burner or old gas ring

Note: VENT OFF GAS FOR FIRST TWO WEEKS (as the first gases produced are not methane.) THEN USE.

RESIDUE → LAND

TABLE OF GAS REQUIREMENTS

cooker	2" burner	11.5 cu.ft/hour or 60 cu.ft. per day for a family. (approx.)
refrigerator	18"x18"x18"	3 cu.ft / hour
hot water	1 bathfull	12 cu.ft.
light	1 mantle	3 cu.ft / hour
engine	per horse power	18 cu.ft./hour

after Ram Bux Singh + Gotaas.

GAS YIELD at different TEMPERATURES

°F	cu.ft. of gas per day per ton of dung.	months.
60	5	12
70	11	6
80	22	3
85	35	2
90	52	1½
✳ 95	70	1

✳ optimum.

after Gotaas.

A methane digestor is worth having for more reasons than gas production alone; ───

    i) The amount of nitrogen in the effluent is stabilised and actually increased. This means that the value of the residue as a fertiliser is greatly enhanced.

    ii) Evil smelling excreta is transformed into sweet smelling fertiliser.

    iii) Weed seeds and disease carrying virus and pathogens are destroyed after 30 days detention in the composter at optimum conditions

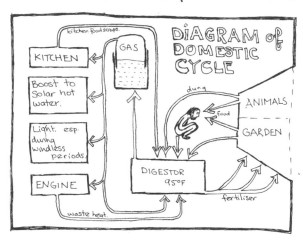

DIAGRAM of DOMESTIC CYCLE

Much anaerobic digestor experience, on a large scale, has been gained by the Local authorities who use this method to process their sewage. A few use the methane produced to run the plant eg. Nottingham + Crossness (S.E. London.) In the recent past Croydon ran a fleet of municipal vehicles on the gas produced from the excreta of the local populace.

It has been estimated that one cow can produce a petrol equivalent in methane of between 2½ and ½ gallons per week.

DESIGN CONSIDERATIONS

1. The bacterialogical process of digestion that produces methane is essentially **ANÆROBIC**. That is, without air. This is most easily arranged by having the digestion take place under water in a sealed tank.

2. Temperature. This is perhaps the most critical factor for whilst the garden compost heap (aerobic) will produce heat (exothermic) the anaerobic process is endothermic ie. absorbs heat from its surroundings. The optimum temperature is 95°F

For temperate regions such as Britain this means it is necessary to supply heat to the digestor tank for most of the year to obtain worthwhile gas yields. Heat conditions should also be steady to give best conditions for the bacteria so temperature controls of some kind are necessary. The heat source may be; ───

    a) Part of the methane that is produced may heat water that is circulated either within the tank in pipes or around the tank as a water-jacket. Alternatively steam may be injected into the digestor tank (this has particular advantages to do with mixing discussed later) The methane used to heat a well insulated tank will be about 30% of the methane produced in average British conditions. Thermostatic temperature control is essential as sudden drops in temperature will adversely effect the acid/alkaline balance (discussed later.)

DESIGN CONSIDERATIONS continued.

2. Temperature (heat sources.)

    b. The sun may be used to heat water (see solar section.) which is circulated around the tank. This method cannot be relied upon to produce high enough temperatures regularly in the winter without another suitable stand-by heat source.

    c. A small heat pump could be used. (see machine section.)

    d. The coolant of a stationary engine may be circulated within the tank. Particularly suitable where the gas produced is being used to drive such an engine to generate electricity or do other work.

    e. Aerobic (+ exothermic) compost / dung heap piled up around the tank will supply both insulation and heat, but it is difficult to control. Method often used by French peasants.

    f. Waste hot water may be circulated around the tank before being disposed of. eg. domestic waste water from baths, washing up etc.

    g. Electrical heating coils (of the type used as 'immersion heaters' with a built in thermostat.) may be used where there is a source of electricity (eg wind.) This kind of heater is useful as a back-up to one of the other less reliable heat sources mentioned above.

INSULATION is ESSENTIAL in our climate. Straw is the cheapest but polystyrene (expanded) is the most effective if you can afford it. Various insulation materials are briefly tabulated in survival scrapbook 1 SHELTER.

3. Input. Different sources recommend varying amounts of water with the solid charge. For ease of handling a 10% dry matter slurry is recommended by Ram Bux Singh of India. However mr Howard Jones of Carmarthen Argricultural college recommends 3% dry weight arguing that this gives a more stable medium for the bacteria although the tank has to be larger. The solids mixture put in may consist of up to about 50% vegetable matter with the dung. This should be chopped up as fibrous plant matter will clog up the digestor. Straw litter may be chaffed to 1½" lengths. Vegetable matter will require more agitation than a mainly dung mix. It will also improve the digestion of veg. material if high carbon content items, such as straw, are soaked with urine which has a high nitrogen content as the carbon/nitrogen ratio is critical to the process.

To feed the mixture into the tank one may use a simple hand operated sludge pump (see below) or a 4" gravity feed pipe. By putting shut off taps at strategic places one pump can be used to pump slurry into the digestor, remove old charge and even circulate and thus mix the slurry.

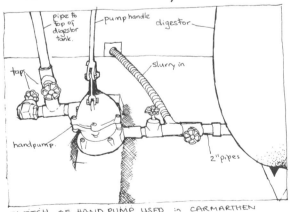

SKETCH OF HAND PUMP USED in CARMARTHEN COLLEGE of AGRICULTURE'S APPARATUS.

see sketch of complete apparatus BIO-GAS 6.

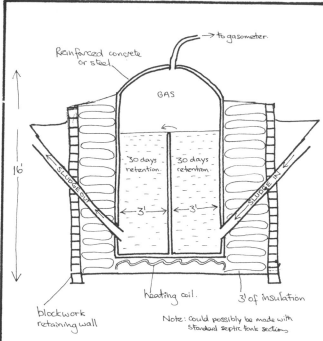

Ram Bux Singh Type.

Reinforced concrete or steel.

→ to gasometer.

GAS

16'

30 days retention | 30 days retention

3' | 3'

SLUDGE OUT

SLUDGE IN

heating coil.

3' of insulation

blockwork retaining wall

Note: could possibly be made with standard septic tank sections

---

Graham Caine with Thames Polytechnic.
'STREET FARM HOUSE'

plumbing connections to sinks + shower

2" vent

agitator

squatting position toilet seat

½" pipe to gasometer

GAS

1" pipe to algae tank

insulation

½" pipes to solar collector.

¼" net

The effluent is used as a nutrient solution for algae. These are then digested in a simpler tank at a higher temperature of 110°F.
STILL IN EXPERIMENTAL STAGES. (summer '73)

Gasholder

A minimum of 70 cu.ft. storage is recommended.

Note: Heavy drums may need counterweights so that too great a back pressure is not built up.

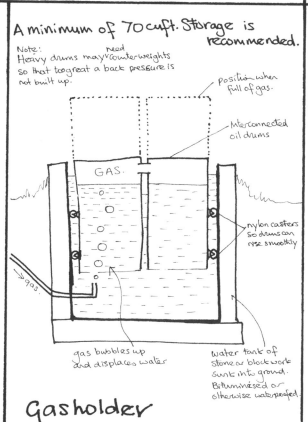

position when full of gas.

Interconnected oil drums

GAS.

nylon casters so drums can rise smoothly

→ gas.

gas bubbles up and displaces water

water tank of stone or blockwork sunk into ground. Bituminised or otherwise waterproofed.

Wright + Rain Ltd. (Fry designer.)

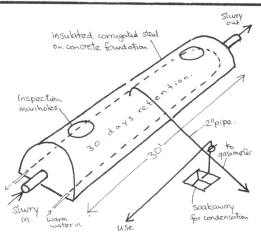

insulated corrugated steel on concrete foundation

Slurry out

inspection manholes

30 days retention.

2" pipe.

to gasometer

Slurry in.

warm water in.

30'

use

soakaway for condensation

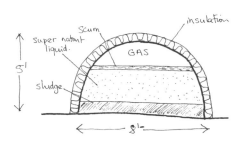

Scum

insulation

super natant liquid.

GAS

5'

sludge

8'

Prototype once made and demonstrated for marketing in Britain.

BIO-GAS ⑤

DESIGN CONSIDERATIONS
continued......

4. Process Progress. to start the process off well it is best to seed the first mixture with an inoculum from an existing plant. This may be obtained from a nearby sewage works or if this is not possible from the surface of a stagnant pool or slow moving stream.

Two main types of digestor may be used. The first is loaded with a full charge, sealed, digested for the required period (see table BIO GAS3) and then removed. This has the disadvantage of intermittent gas production and irregular loading (and therefore disposal.) of slurry and the possible advantage of simplicity. A useful type for the digestion of fibrous vegetable material as handling difficulties are reduced.

The second is loaded with a full charge then continuously loaded and discharged. The tank is designed to retain the charge for the required period (eg. 30 days minimum at 95°F.)

According to Singh the charge gets lighter for the first 30 days and then becomes heavier so inlets and outlets must be placed accordingly, depending on design of tank and retention period.

As we go to press it is suggested that a diverse input into a digestor will encourage a stable microfloral development. This sounds very reason-able so try putting in all sorts of organic wastes even if they don't supply bulk (domestic wastes) Alph moorcroft.

5. Scumming. In a digestor tank with a small liquid surface area a thick fibrous scum may form which inhibits the process. This scum may be avoided by either having a much larger surface area or by agitating the mixture. Mixing the contents by agitation also improves fermentation. The agitation may be either mechanical (steel rod) or by pumping effluent or recirculating gas or injecting steam. Agitation is usually done for about 15 minutes each day.

6. PH or acidity. Too acid conditions sometimes form and inhibit the process. This is most often caused by;
 * high loading rates.
 * drop in temperature.
 * scum formation.

Dilution or the careful addition of lime may help if acidity occurs. Simplest acidity test is Litmus paper, ask your chemist. Optimum pH value is between 7-8. (near neutral)

7. Sulphur products. The first two weeks gas production is run off as it is too adulterated to be useful, the first part of the process (whilst air is still present) being aerobic. After two weeks hydrogen sulphide may still be produced but may be removed by bubbling through lime water or with an 'iron oxide' scrubber.' Some sources suggest that the small amount of hydrogen sulphide that is likely to be produced is not very troublesome when the gas is being used on a small scale.

BIO GAS 5

BIO-GAS 6

EXPERIMENTAL METHANE PRODUCER
at CARMARTHEN COLLEGE OF AGRICULTURE. CYMRU (WALES)

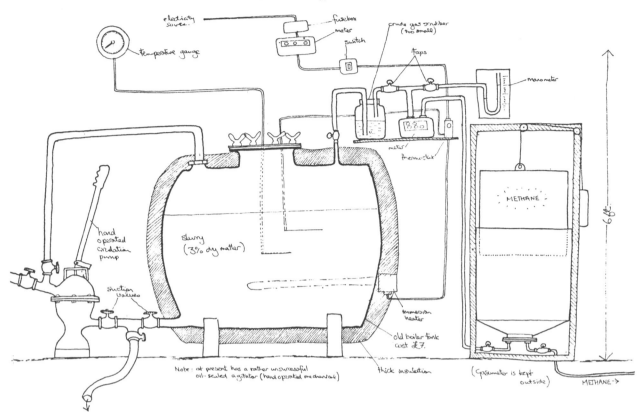

Note: at present has a rather unsuccessful oil-sealed agitator (hand operated mechanical)

(gasometer is kept outside)

METHANE →

Size of Plant is determined by multiplying the average volume of slurry for gas needs per day × the number of days in the cycle. 72 lbs of dung occupies approx. 1 cu.ft. One lb of dung produces one cuft. of gas. Remember an, at least, equal quantity of water must be added. A domestic plant for a couple of cows + assorted humans and small animals needs a plant of approx. 100 cuft. Precast concrete septic tanks may be suitable for conversion, are about the right size, cost about £100 for a basic kit.

✳ For some details of privy design see *Survival Scrapbook Food*. section on disposal.

✳ Storage by compression is only possible if <u>all</u> air is first removed. (or explosion will occur.) At present simple method not known(?)

✳ Avoid putting detergents or substances that might upset the bacterialogical action into the digestor.

✳ Methane is an odourless, heavier than air gas. As a protection against leaks and possible explosions odourise the gas with tetrahydrothiosphene so leaks can be detected.

✳ Pressurising gas in the gasholder by adding weights or by using heavy gasometer drums can inhibit gas production by causing a back pressure. Storage tanks may have to be counterbalanced.

✳ The possibilies of composting a mixture with only a small amount of excreta + the usual domestic + garden degradable wastes have not been fully investigated yet. Graham Caines digestor in the street farmhouse is experimenting with such a situation.

BIO GAS 6

WATER ～～～～～

Moving water can be used in many ways; as a source of power or as a source of low temperature heat (heat pump.)

The 3 main classes of water wheel are illustrated overleaf. These are: The vertical waterwheel (commonly seen picturesque) The reaction wheel in which a jet of water is directed onto blades or buckets and the Impulse wheel in which buckets around the circumference of the wheel are simultaneously filled by water that continuously flows into them through conduits called chutes or guides.

There are many variations possible within these 3 classes.

Ordinary vertical wheels have been almost entirely superseded by turbines and impulsewheels.

In most situations the main work in constructing a water power plant is not in the wheel but in arranging for a suitable fall of water.

There are two main ways of doing this: Damming the valley down which the stream flows. (section on dams in S.S. Food.) or making a 'mill race' along the side of the valley. This aqueduct will usually join the stream ¼ to ½ a mile above the mill wheel and being fairly level relative to the stream will give the required fall of between 10-20 feet. Both methods require considerable constructional or excavation works and are often severly limited by our present system of land ownership.

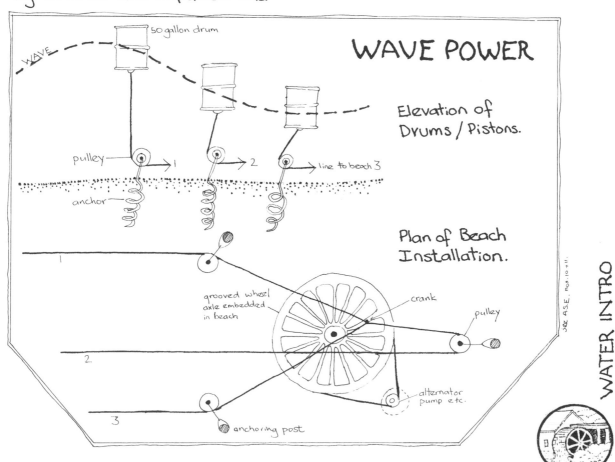

WAVE POWER

50 gallon drum

WAVE

Elevation of Drums / Pistons.

pulley

line to beach 3

anchor

Plan of Beach Installation.

grooved wheel axle embedded in beach

crank

pulley

alternator pump etc.

anchoring post

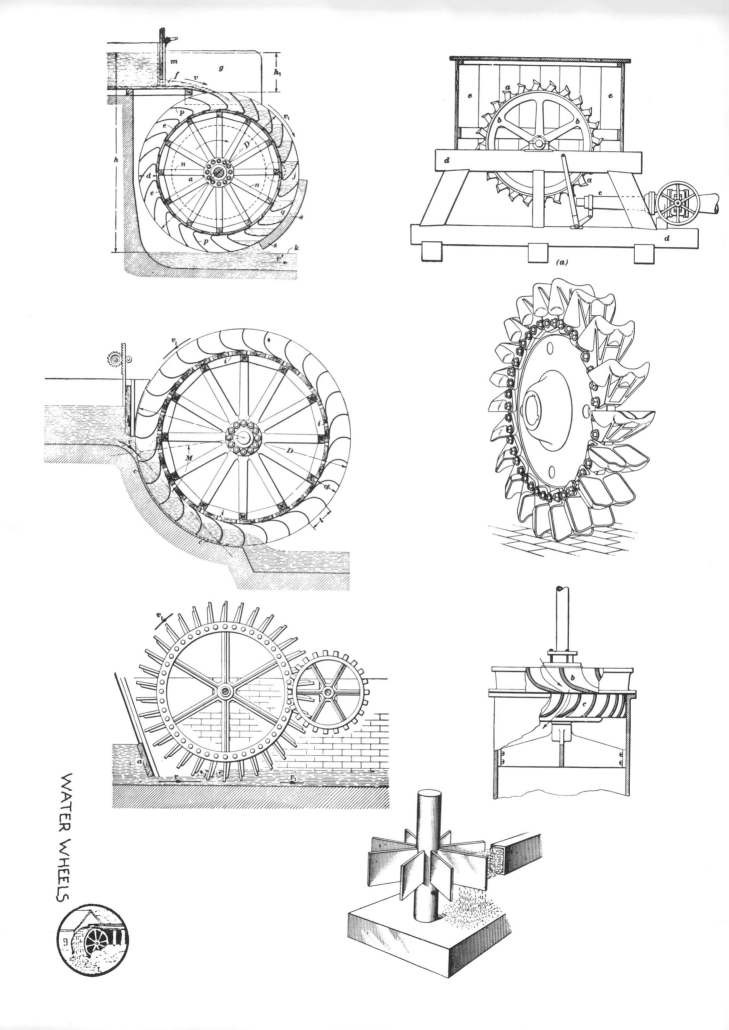

(a)

A home-constructed water power plant on a Welsh farm.
Brynog, Felinfach, Cardiganshire.

inexpensive materials—an old binder wheel, and the axle shafting
and gearing from an old Deering mowing machine.

The water wheel itself is the main driving wheel of the
binder which has a normal rim width of 9" was extended
by 4" either side with timber packing. The outer segments
form the sides of 20 troughs into which the water is
directed. The roller 'steel ball' bearings were knocked out
and a solid shaft was keyed into the hub. This was
then set in bearings mounted on a reinforced concrete
waterway. The solid shaft is joined to the old axle by
a universal coupling. From the axle the drive continues at
right angles to drive a 14" pulley which drives the 4"
pulley of the 35 volt dynamo with a flat belt. The
step up gearing of the pulley and the axle ensure +650rpm
for the dynamo in normal stream flow.

Water power plant on a Scottish farm made from
old cart wheels and a motor car dynamo.

The water-wheel is made of two
cart-wheels. (4 ft in diameter)
Fourteen buckets have been formed
between these. The wheel is mounted
on an axle of iron piping operating
in bearings of wood.
The water shoots the buckets at only
about 7 inches from the bottom of the
wheel (I would have thought it would have
worked better entering 3/4 of the way up?)
The wheel speed is stepped up in the ratio
of 19 to 1 through gears to drive a
motor-car dynamo, mounted on a
framework at the side.
When water is in good supply the plant
operates five lights and works a pump
via a motor-car battery 100 yds away
in a barn.

IMPROVISE

WATER POWER

Even a small stream may be able to supply a lot of power if you are in a position to exploit it. For example a stream with 30 cu.ft. per minute flow and falling 30ft is able to provide about 1½ kwh.

<u>To Estimate Stream Flow</u> you must estimate the average width depth and speed of the stream. (Estimate speed using weighted wooden strips that are submerged 2/3 of their height and measure average distances travelled in one minute.) The depth, width, distance and the constant 0·8 are then multiplied together to give an approximate flow in cu.ft. per minute. Enquire about constancy of flow throughout the year from other people who have lived next to the stream for some years.

Another method for small streams is to direct all the water for a short period (say 10 seconds.) into a reservoir or container. This water is then immediately transferred to a regular rectangular container from which the volume and thus stream flow is calculated. Note: Of course a cylinderical drum may be used instead of a rectangular container if this is more convenient.

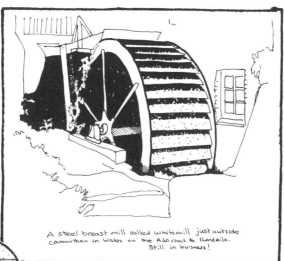

A steel breast mill called Whitemill just outside Carmarthen in Wales on the A40 road to Llandeilo. Still in buisness!

HOME MADE PELTON

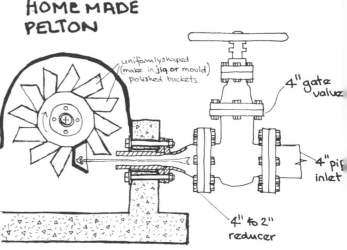

uniformly shaped (make in jig or mould) polished buckets

4" gate value

4" pipe inlet

4" to 2" reducer

Mother Earth News.

HEAD	FLOW	POWER
25ft.	26 cu.ft. per.min	1.0 h.p.
30	30 " "	1·3
40	36 " "	2·0
50	40 " "	2·8
60	44 " "	3·75

POWER AVAILABLE FROM A SMALL TURBINE : as shown above.

Note: The water should be brought from its high reservoir to the turbine in pipes that have as few corners as possible. When a corner is necessary it should be gradual and smooth. (this is to reduce turbulence.)

Overshot wheel Power

$$Power = 0.001285 \times Q \times H$$
in horse power

Q = cu.ft. of water per minute.
H = height of useful fall in feet.

As a big wheel moves slowly it is not as important to have it carefully balanced or with such fine bearings as a turbine, although they must be kept well lubricated.

With a 5ft head a 10ft wheel will give about ½ h.p. at 10 r.p.m. per foot width of bucket filled. (bucket 8" deep × 22 in number.)

❃ The comparative efficiency of a turbine and overshot wheel is approx. 8 : 6.

A waterwheel is generally simpler to maintain than a windmill of equivalent output. ❃

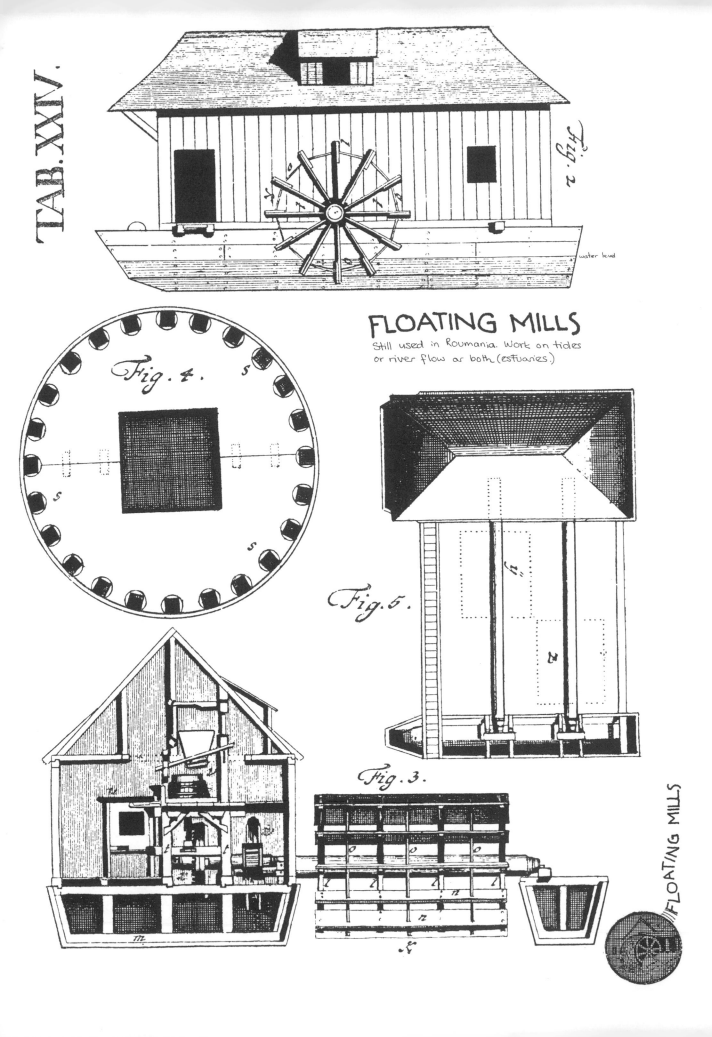

TAB.XXIV.

Fig. 1.

water level

FLOATING MILLS

Still used in Roumania. Work on tides
or river flow or both (estuaries.)

Fig. 4.

Fig. 5.

Fig. 3.

FLOATING MILLS

TIDAL MILLS

From as early as the 11th century tide-mills were erected wherever suitable sites could be found. There are still a few tidal mills in Britain e.g. at Woodbridge in Suffolk. and Carew in Pembroke.

Only on a large scale do they supply power that is economically competitive with traditionally fuelled power stations. (using capitalist criteria.) An example of such a large scheme is the Rance scheme in North France which delivers 60 million kWh per year. However small community sized units are worth building on a limited number of sites that are shaped in such a way that a minimum of barrage building will trap a large reservoir.

Tides are raised every 25 hours or so in two ways.

i) The water directly under the moon is pulled upward by gravitational attraction (scientific mystery.)

ii) On the opposite side of the earth another tide is raised by centrifugal force.

The two tides are similar on the open ocean being about 16 inches. This is magnified by the topography of local coastline especially in estuaries and channels.

A rough guide to the potential of a of a particular location is given by the formula $\frac{Ah}{l}$ where A is the impounded area, h is the mean range of tide and l is the length of barrage necessary. A large impounded area, great tidal range of height and a short barrage are all conducive to low cost and high power potential.

Note: With the Siphon turbine arrangement (see bottom left.) the bulb may be simply maintained as it is above water level. Other submerged types need sluice gates to make them accessible. These bulb turbines are suitable for medium scale power supply giving between 100 — 1000 Kwh.

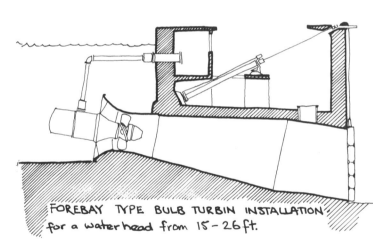

FOREBAY TYPE BULB TURBIN INSTALLATION:
for a water head from 15 - 26 ft.

SIPHON TYPE BULB
for water head of 10 - 15 ft. only.

Note: water level switches operating solenoid value and priming pump make automatic operation easy.

Machines have been investigated that extract power from wave motion. They have similar principles of operation to The 'Tree Pump' see wind section. Small, powerful wave motion is translated into faster motion with the use of blocks usually driving a fly wheel via a ratchet drive. As with tides more potential in situations in which natural coast forms amplify wave height by funneling effects. etc.

TIDAL MILLS

STORAGE ONE

When using unreliable and intermittent sources of free income energy such as sun and wind the storage of energy gained is essential if the activities that rely on such energies are not to be severely curtailed during periods of 'drought'. Often there is a choice between getting a reasonably good storage system together and changing your life style to accomodate the intermittent energy supply.

There are 3 main types of storage:—

i) Heat Storage: in a stable material with a reasonably high thermal capacity. eg water + rocks.

ii) Chemical: Either a reversible reaction that can be made to give back what you put in (usually electricity) or a stable fuel (eg. methane.)

iii) Mechanical Storage: By creating a potential energy that may be retrieved in a convenient manner eg. pumping water up to a higher level and letting in fall through a turbine or compressing air and releasing it to drive a turbine.

The method(s) of storage chosen will depend on the type of incoming energy and the situation in which you find yourself. If, for instance, energy is being collected from the sun it is likely that heat storage will be most convenient. If, however, the energy is from the wind then a mechanical or chemical storage would probably be best.

i) Heat Storage: Insulation is a critical factor. High temperature storage means you can store a lot of heat in a small space but insulation will be a problem. It is more practical to store at reasonably low temperature on a domestic scale (about the heat of hot washing water.) Storage of water in well insulated tanks under a dwelling is a commonly used form of storage. Old cellars may be simply converted. see insulation notes in S.S.I. shelter. It is less costly to store heat in fist size rocks, by passing hot air between them, because no watertight tanks are necessary. see solar section : AIR COLLECTOR.

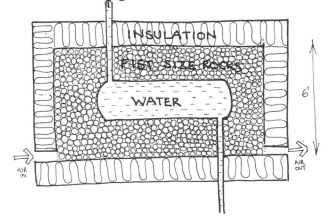

Water circulates through a simple tank heat exchanger by natural convection if possible so a pump is not necessary.

✳ The heat capacity of water may be raised by four times by adding sodium sulphate (The thermic change from the hydrated to unhydrated salt occurs at 90°F.)

✳ David Stabb suggests augering deep holes into the ground and storing heat in the earth. Water piped into these holes could take heat down and bring it up as desired.

STORAGE 2 MECHANICAL.

Mechanical Storage: Water.

The simplest system would seem to be that of pumping water up to a higher level; but it needs 96,900 gallons falling one metre to produce one kilo watt hour of power so its not much good thinking of a roof tank or tower if you want to store appreciable amounts of energy. 'Costs' would be prohibitive. If however you were in a situation of having a natural change of level (eg a hill.) up which you could cheaply pump water (see S.S. Food for page on Pumps.) and on top of which you could simply store it (eg. a lake.) then this method is feasible.

idea: Dig a well. Pump water up from the well with a wind pump etc. Store water in a lake on the surface. Then in times of energy shortage let water fall back into well to drive a turbine at the bottom of the well. The turbine drives a generator. Electrical energy travels up out of the well with little effort. suggested by manjeet.

Another limitation to this kind of storage might be the low efficiency of small scale pumps (approx 30%)

Lifting weights has similar but greater limitations. Almost 800,000 lbs needs to be raised one metre to produced one kilowatt when lowered. Still if you've got some big rocks around you might be able to devize something.?

Mechanical Storage : Air.

Compressing air needs large (∴ expensive) tanks in order to store a useful amount of energy. Very high pressures require smaller containers but they need to be very strong, compressor more expensive and it's more dangerous. You may be able to get cheap secondhand pressure tanks, but be careful, have it checked out thoroughly, compressed air can be very dangerous.

idea: needs developing. An underground tank is given an airtight lining (P.V.C. bag?) Strength of tank lies in the enormous mass of earth surrounding it. Might be low cost.

Almost any kind of tool may be driven by compressed air turbine. Most rotary vane type air driven motors are lighter and more reliable than their electricity driven equivalent. eg. They cannot burn out and they are easily reversed.

AIR DRILLS

Mechanical Storage: Kinetic Inertia.

A flywheel with 100 lbs at the rim travelling at 1000 ft per sec. (rim speed.) could store over ½ kilowatt Also useful to smooth out short term fluctuations of energy income (eg. wind gusts) Storage capacity / weight ratio is comparable with small car batteries !

STORAGE 3 ELECTRICAL

The automobile battery is invariably of the lead/sulphuric acid type. It consists of an electrode of lead and another of lead oxide immersed in sulphuric acid. The principles of such batteries are well described in common reference books. *e.g. How Things Work.* Because of their rough life auto batteries have a useful life of only about 2 years. Other designs for more stable conditions may have a ten year life. Iron/nickel alkaline batteries and nickel/cadmium batteries are more efficient and tougher than lead/acid but more expensive.

Apparently the storage batteries made for electrically driven vehicles (milk floats, golf carts etc) are designed to be charged up overnight and drained during the day. These characteristics would suit the storage of intermittent income energies and their likely domestic use.

Lead/acid batteries are damaged by:
  i/ overcharging.
  ii/ over discharge.
  iii/ frost.
Care must be taken if a long life is to be expected

✳ Dagenite manufacture a small battery for use by caravaners. It is included in the Bardic carapac shown on the right →

Electrolysis of Water: an electric current passed between platinum electrodes in water will break the water down into its component parts. This process may be reversed, with high efficiency, hydrogen and oxygen combining to produce water and electricity. This device is called a fuel cell. The process is still somewhat experimental, problems being the short life span of the electrodes and the capital cost of equipment. However hydrogen produced from simple electrolysis may be otherwise used as a fuel, (for conversion of motor car to H_2 see Perris Smogless Auto Association Report called "Hydrogen Car" from P.O. Box 892 Perris CA 92370) or see A.S.E mag 11.

Electricity from a (12 volt) auto battery may be converted to 220 volts AC for using low amp. domestic equipment by using a dynamotor. Cheap ex-service versions are frequently advertised in Exchange and Mart.

If you use a motorcar you can charge another battery whilst you ride around. You will need a special device that will give your car battery priority charge and then when that is fully charged it will switch over to the second. Also charges from mains or perhaps a windmill.

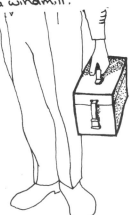

Portability is a strong point. The Carapac is as easy to carry with one hand as a laden shopping basket.

GAS CONVERSION

of a petrol driven internal combustion engine.

You can use propane, butane or methane. Unless you use home-made methane gas it will not be cheaper but it is less pollutive and better for the engine. Gas at any pressure from 5 lbs/sq.in. to 1100 lbs/sq.in. may be used. Gas in lower pressure range needs to be raised to vapourising temperature (above 30°F)

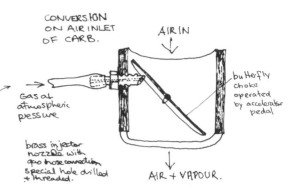

CONVERSION ON AIR INLET OF CARB.

AIR IN

Gas at atmospheric pressure

butterfly choke operated by accelerator pedal

brass injector nozzle with gas hose connection special hole drilled & threaded.

AIR + VAPOUR.

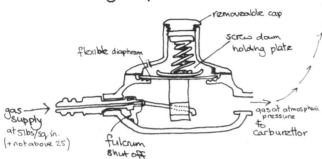

removeable cap

flexible diaphram

screw down holding plate

gas supply at 5lbs/sq.in. (+ not above 25)

fulcrum shut off

gas at atmospheric pressure to carburettor

GAS SUPPLY REGULATOR: Make this from a calor gas type 75* regulator. Cut original spring in, about, half. Buy several springs and find best length for your engine. Adjust on idle. Gas at over 25 lbs/sq.in needs a primary regular (standard) to take the gas down to 5 lbs/sq.in before the modified regulator.

* in USA. use BEAM regulator.

Most conversions make use of bottle gas but large refillable tanks could be used. Small pressure bottles have too little surface area (of liquified gas) to give enough gas vapour in cold weather. Large tanks do not have this disadvantage.

Note 1. SAFETY. Gas bottles sometimes explode. Gas Taxis in London have 1/4" steel plate between passangers + gas bottles.

Note 2. A 15% diesel / 85% methane mixture can be used in a diesel engine. (H.A. Mackrill. Worcester Authority Engineer 1950s)

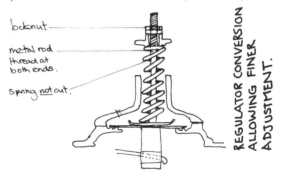

locknut

metal rod thread at both ends.

spring not cut.

REGULATOR CONVERSION ALLOWING FINER ADJUSTMENT.

A wartime automobile gas bag. Suitable for Home-made Methane.

The Motor Manual Temple Press 1943

GENERATORS

The two most versatile machines ever produced are probably the internal combustion engine and the electric motor (and its reverse the electrical generator or dynamo)

A type of the I.C. engine that demonstrates this versatility in one power unit is the smallholders cultivator or garden tiller. This unit may be used to power on extra-ordinary range of activities. The same is true of the electric motor in the form of a hand power drill. A combination of the fuel engine and the dynamo gives us ther portable electricity production unit of the small generator.

Most petrol generators could be fairly simply converted to methane gas.

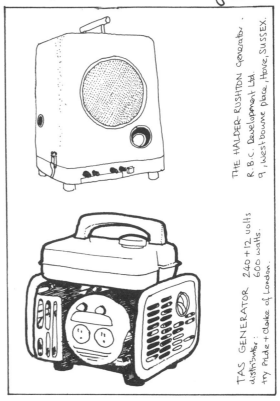

THE HALDER-RUSHTON Generator.
R.B.C. Development Ltd.
9, Westbourne place, Hove, SUSSEX.

TAS GENERATOR. 240 + 12 volts 600 watts.
distributor:
try Pride + Clarke of London.

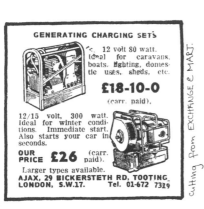

GENERATING CHARGING SETS

12 volt 80 watt. Ideal for caravans, boats. lighting, domestic uses, sheds, etc.

£18-10-0
(carr. paid),

12/15 volt, 300 watt. Ideal for winter conditions. Immediate start. Also starts your car in seconds.

OUR PRICE **£26** (carr. paid).

Larger types available.
AJAX, 29 BICKERSTETH RD, TOOTING. LONDON, S.W.17. Tel. 01-672 7319

Cutting from EXCHANGE & MART.

GENERATORS ALSO MADE BY :—

✳ R.A. Lister & Co Dursley, Gloucester. big types — press button start etc.

✳ E & M Powerplant Ltd. Magnate Works, Whitehouse road, Ipswich, Suffolk.

✳ LUCAS electrical. 12v dc. (a gas converted model was available.) Take off point for power tool flexible drive.

✳ Raynar + Co. Five Acres garden centre, Chichester. ?

✳ Home light. Grimstead + co. 263 Barking road. London E.6. (distributor)

✳ HONDA. generally more versatile and cheaper than other makes, may be less reliable and robust than other types — difficult to assess.
Home manufacturers find it difficult to compete with this Japanese firm. see below

E300E

Compact, easily portable generator providing electricity wherever and whenever it is required. Generating AC or DC this unit will power most home and workshop appliances up to 300 Watts consumption and will charge car or boat batteries.

£110 approx.

E4000E

Largest unit in the generator range providing both AC and DC simultaneously. Has a continuous rated output of 3½ kw and has many applications for both the industrial and domestic field or as stand-by power. Charges 12 or 24 volt batteries. GD100 diesel engine, 4 kw max. AC 8.4 amps DC.

£600 approx.

ELECTRIC GENERATORS

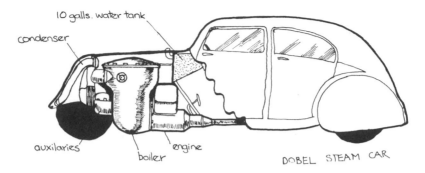

10 galls. water tank

condenser

auxilaries

boiler

engine

DOBEL STEAM CAR

STEAM ENGINES

In 1906 Stanleys Steam car set a new world speed record of 127.5 m.p.h. Modern steam engines are almost silent, are more reliable than the internal combustion engine and are only 1/20 as pollutive in terms of noxious gas emission. Steam is raised from cold in less than one minute with a flash boiler. No clutch or gearing are necessary for variable power applications. i.e. motor cars. 'Car engine revs at 900 r.p.m. at 60 mph. This low engine speed makes the unit ALMOST EVERLASTING. Running costs— 20 m.p.g. at 50 m.p.h. but burns almost any fuel. Simple relatively inefficient types may be homemade.

mainly from _Practical Motorists Encyclopaedia F.J. Camm. Newnes 1952_

RICARDO: After the last World War the National Research + Development Council commisioned messers Ricardo and Company (1927) Ltd. to develop a small multi fuel (peat, wood etc) prime mover that could supply power on a domestic scale. Prototypes were successful but it dissappeared. where? It looked like the sketch here →

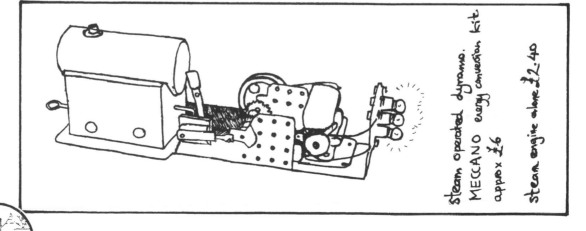

steam operated dynamo. MECCANO energy convertion kit appox £6

steam engine alone £2.40

HEAT PUMP

A Heat pump has the same apparatus as a refrigerator but it works in reverse, absorbing heat at low temperature and emitting it elsewhere at high temperature. A description that illustrates the principle is on the page about 'the production of cold by solar heat.' Detail descriptions of the principles involved are contained in many text books. see 'How Things Work.'

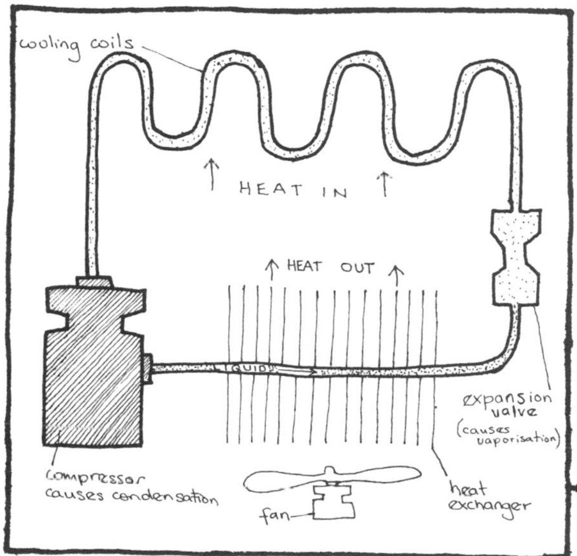

A good heat source is a stream (which may be at about 10°C) Heat taken from the running water is then pumped up to a higher temperature of 60°-70°C. About one kilowatt (kw) of electricity operating the compressor/pump will give 3 or 4 kilowatts of heat. The compressor could be driven from batteries charged by wind or water power. BRAD a research community in Montgomeryshire have a heat pump compressor unit made by Frigidaire bought secondhand but reconditioned. It was originally made to serve a cool storage room or some such. In this case heat exchangers are being specially made to suit but could probably be found secondhand. see The Journal of the Industrial Materials, Recovery Assn. It is hoped the set will provide up to 7 kw of heat continuously for a household of 15 people.

cooling coils

HEAT IN

HEAT OUT

liquid

expansion valve (causes vaporisation)

compressor causes condensation

fan

heat exchanger

❄ This diagram illustrates the basic system. The liquid that is pumped around, the refrigerant, has a low boiling point. examples of common refrigerants are ammonia, ethyl chloride and freon. The heat source for the cooling coils may be solar radiation, water, air or the earth. Anything that can keep supplying as much heat as you need. (Even if it is at a low temperature!)

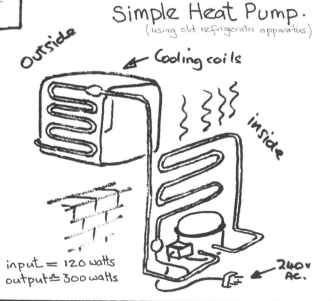

Simple Heat Pump.
(using old refrigerator apparatus.)

Outside

← Cooling coils

inside

input = 120 watts
output ≃ 300 watts

240v AC.

Tony Williams.

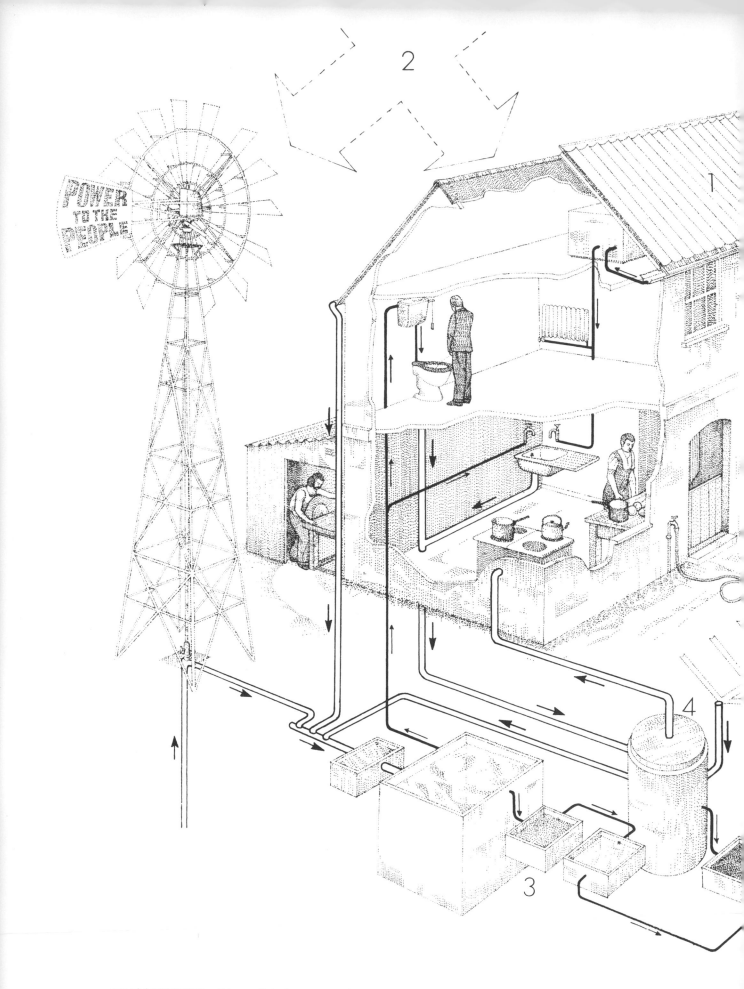

POWER TO THE PEOPLE

2

1

4

3

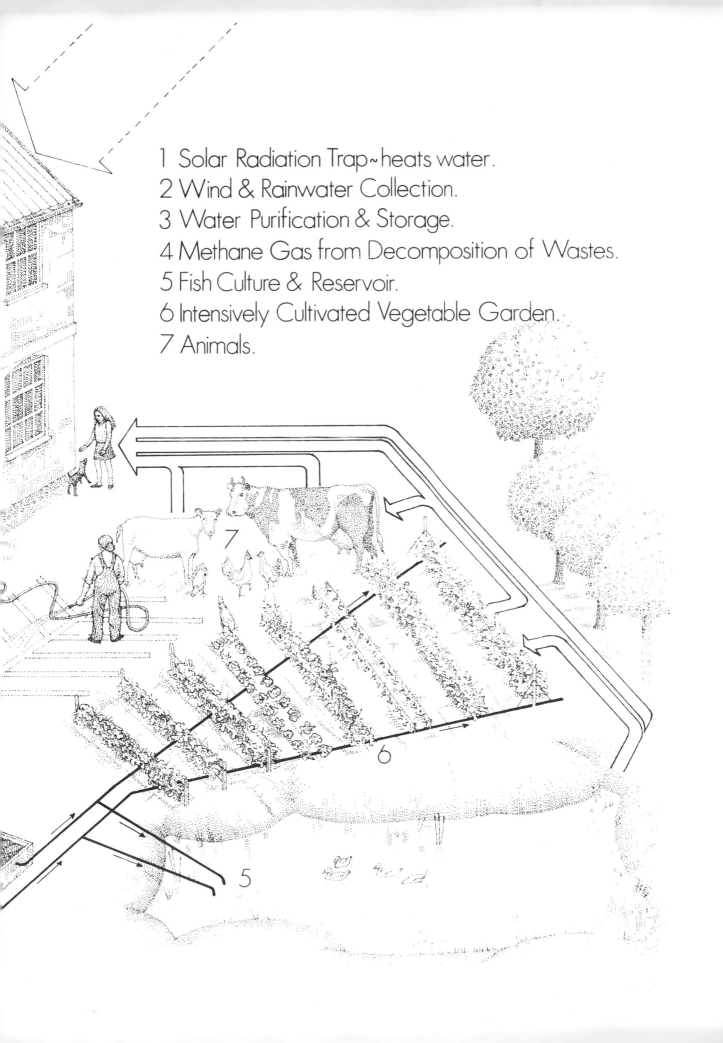

1 Solar Radiation Trap~heats water.
2 Wind & Rainwater Collection.
3 Water Purification & Storage.
4 Methane Gas from Decomposition of Wastes.
5 Fish Culture & Reservoir.
6 Intensively Cultivated Vegetable Garden.
7 Animals.

STREET FARMHOUSE

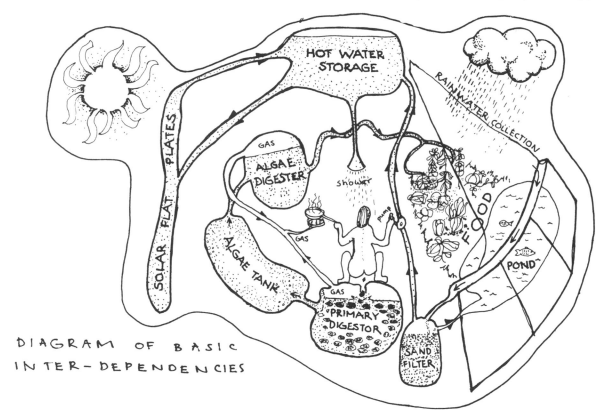

HOT WATER STORAGE

RAINWATER COLLECTION

SOLAR FLAT PLATES

GAS
ALGAE DIGESTER

SHOWER

GAS

ALGAE TANK

FOOD

POND

GAS
PRIMARY DIGESTOR

SAND FILTER

DIAGRAM OF BASIC INTER-DEPENDENCIES

WITHIN THE STREET FARMHOUSE ALL ORGANIC MATTER IS RECYCLED TO RECONSTITUTE FOOD AND RELEASE ENERGY IN THE FORM OF GAS FOR COOKING. RAINWATER IS COLLECTED AND FILTERED TO PROVIDE DRINKING AND WASHING WATER, WITH DOMESTIC HOT WATER BEING OBTAINED FROM SIMPLE SOLAR FLAT COLLECTORS ie. RADIATOR PANELS. A WIND ROTOR, SOLAR CONCENTRATING COLLECTOR, HEAT PUMP AND VARIOUS OTHER THINGS ARE AT PRESENT BEING TRIED OUT.
ALL THE PARTS OF THIS EXPERIMENTAL HOUSE ARE SIMPLE, CHEAP AND EASILY PUT TOGETHER WITHOUT SPECIAL SKILLS.
THE REDUCTION OF DEPENDENCE ON THE STATE MEANS A REDUCTION OF THE STATES CONTROL OVER INDIVIDUALS REPLACING IT WITH A DEPENDENCE ON THE NATURAL ENVIRONMENT BRINGING PEOPLE BACK INTO RECOGNISABLE RELATIONSHIPS OF INTERDEPENDENCE RATHER THAN OBSCURE OPERATIONS WITHIN MASS, ALIENATING, CENTRALISED SYSTEMS.

for more details of a practical and theoretical nature send S.A.E. to STREET FARMHOUSE, Kidbrooke lane, Eltham, LONDON. S.E.9.

ANIMAL POWER

DONKEY WHEEL at Hinton, Wiltshire. Demolished in 1908.

Dog and sheep churning butter

3 Let Fido carry his own food • Sturdy nylon, waterproof zippered panniers • Leather reinforced corners.

CRUELTY A CRITICAL CONCEPTUAL CONFUSION?

from a photograph by Will F Taylor

ELEPHANT LOADING TIMBER

ANIMAL POWER 1

McCORMICK'S PATENT AMERICAN REAPER.

1920's ———— 2,000,000 workhorses in England. 1971 ———— 2000 shire workhorses. TIMES 24/11/71.

Animals as a Heat Source: In the Alps the houses are often designed so that the living quarters are over the stables. In winter when the animals must be stabled all the time, because of the snow, their body heat helps to keep the house warm. This is greatly helped by the good insulation afforded by keeping the hay stored in a very large 'attic' above and very thick stone side walls. In addition the firewood, for the centrally placed cooking and heating stove, is stored by leaning it against the walls of the house under the protecting roof eaves. This improves the wall insulation even more. Similar principles apply in the traditional Welsh Longhouse.

Glo worms and Fireflies
Pyrophorus, the most brightly luminous animal known, was used by West Indians in place of candles in their huts. Native girls used the insect for decoration in the hair and tied them to their feet to light up forest paths at night.

The most elaborate organic flashing is seen in the fireflies of Burma + Thailand. These will collect in thousands on the leaves of every tree for a distance of several hundred yards and then proceed to flash in unison. Their synchronous pulsation may continue hour after hour, night after night, for weeks or even months on end.

extract from *The Light of Glowworms and Fireflies* Science News 12 Penguin. 1940's by Dr. V.B. Wigglesworth. F.R.S.

* We may note that certain complete animals are used as fuel and lighting. eg. The Stormy Petrel and Candlefish which being rich in fat burns without a wick
* The beetle, Elateridae 'The firefly' allows reading to be done by the light of one insect. Used in American Indian and Chinese festivities as illumination.

Note: One cow gives off 20,000 calories of heat per day.

sweet smelling hay cut from high mountain pastures. includes many herbs.

3ft thick stone + mud walls

firewood.

cattle + goats

ground slopes up

ANIMAL POWER 2

HUMAN MUSCLE

The human body is not as powerful as many animals but aided by the large brain..... the human body is capable of devising ingenious tools to increase its speed, power or reach. The brain also enables these tools to be used, after much practice, with great delicacy and skill.

Of course, everybody knows all this but it is amazing how little people think about some basic problem before giving up or calling in a specialist.

One of the best tools for converting human muscle power into another useful form is the modern bicycle. A version of this tool which may be used to drive a great variety of things such as lathe, butterchurn, mill or mixer is shown overleaf.

The body itself is capable of developing super normal qualities under special guidance from the brain. The mystic disciplines of asceticism and concentration resulted in some extremes of physiological control.

A Chinese farmer's children turning a stone roller which grinds grain into flour

One instance that seems of a relatively practical nature is of the Yogi in the snow, who would sit near naked for hours or even days in ludicrously cold conditions. I wonder if a popular culture could develop higher degrees of control? Some people in temperate regions wear very little clothing. Also an article in 'Childrens Rights mag.' reports on a couple of kids who were given a complete choice in their clothing, from an early age, and chose to wear very little. They seemed able to control their bodily heat to much greater extent than usual + were tougher getting few colds and so on.

DYNAPOD

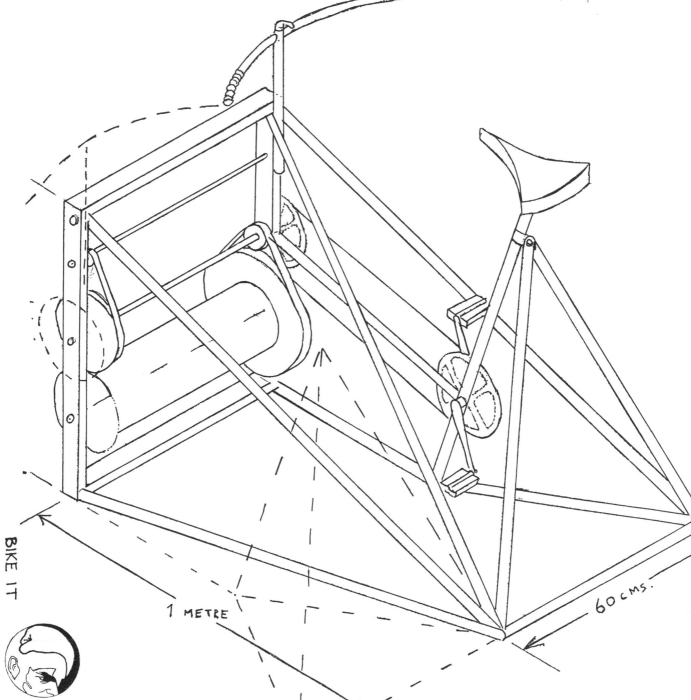

BIKE IT

1 METRE

60 CMS.

MIND ENERGY

The energy involved in controlling any function is usually minute compared with the amount of energy used to actually power the function. This energy moves information from an 'area' that recognises need to other areas that may do something about it. Although the energies involved here are small they are critical. Used with care and wisdom they can reduce the larger energies necessary for the action or use them more effectively. In fact in some areas brute force maybe of no use and results can only be achieved through strategic thinking.

It is unfortunate that in the mental/psychic areas of energetics and power most techniques widely used are dangerously institutionalised in such Organisations as Scientology, Divine Light and the Roman Catholic Church.

There are many techniques that may be used to develop, train or energise latent mental powers. I list a good deal below and go on to enlarge on a couple further on.

The danger of such techniques institutionalised is that:

1. There is usually some heirachy in evidence with a top group who have a rake off. (Profit + power.)

2. The devotees are under the power of the organisation rather than being liberated and because of this are subject to the whims and idiosyn--crasies of its policy makers.

3. The ritual aspects of such organisations being formulated to ensure their own prolonged survival are not responsive to the moment. Such dogma tends to condition the mind at a profound level whilst being 'liberating' on the level of a superficial euphoria.

LIST OF SOME TECHNIQUES.

ACETICISM	DIVINING	PAINTING
ALCHEMY	ENDURANCE	PILGRIMAGE
ASTROLOGY	ELECTRIC THERAPY	PRAYER
BREATHING	FASTING	PYSCHEDELICS
CHANTING	FUNG SHUI	I CHING
CONCENTRATION	GAMES	RITUAL
CONJURING	HYPNOTISM	SEX
CONVERSATION	MANTRA	STUDY
DANCING	MARTIAL ARTS	WIZARDRY
DISCIPLINE	MEDITATION	YOGA

SIMPLE PURE MEDITATION

There are various techniques by which good mental conditions for quiet meditation may be obtained. One of the simplest and least gimmicky that I have come across is Vipassana Meditation. (Thai Buddhist derivation) This I will describe as a convenient example having experienced some practice.

Choose a quiet, warm, peaceful place. Begin by sitting comfortably but upright either on a good chair or crosslegged on a cushion. Hands are laid relaxed on the lap. Eyes are closed. Now. Be alert to everything that is happening. For a start watch breathing. Attention should rest on the movement of the abdomen. This sitting and watching breathing should be done for approximately quarter of an hour, twice a day, regularly.

Attention to breathing leads gradually outward and inward to all other perceptions. You will become gradually aware of bodily functionings, thoughts and ideas, emotions, nearby events, air movements and so on. It is said that if you can be clearly aware of —— the arising of a thought, emotion, perception —— its presence and continuing —— its dying away.......... then by knowing the process fully you gain control of it and it loses control of you. Meditation will thus throw off the layers of conditioning that surround your 'normal' conciousness. However in taking ideas about meditation too seriously there is a danger that ideas about what you should achieve will condition your meditation. Confused? Do not be put off, watch the confusion. Losing interest? Watch the loss of interest. Mind wandering?..... dreaming........... watch your attention forming and drifting.
Take nothing for granted.
Relax and be alert.

A Method of Increasing Chi.

Chi is a term for intrinsic energy. It is at the basis of most Eastern Martial Arts especially Tai Chi and Aikido. The development of Chi gives you the pliability of a infant. Accumulated in the tan t'ien (a point just below the navel) and used properly it has the quality of massed wind or water.
A method of 'laying in a store' of Chi in the quickest time is given by John F Gilbey in his book 'Secret Fighting Arts of the World'. _____ Choose a quiet room, with low lighting and set aside fifteen minutes every day.
Sit down comfortably. Relax. Breathe about ten a minute or less. Breath in through nose out through mouth (silently) The tongue should adhere to the roof of the mouth. Cover the right ear lightly with the left hand. Think of only one thing. RELAXATION After five minutes reverse hands. Right hand over left ear _____ for another five minutes. Then a final five with both hands covering both ears. That's all. Expect things to happen after two weeks regular practice.

CHI

WHOEVER YOU VOTED FOR....

.THE GOVERNMENT GOT IN.

HYPNOSIS

The subconcious mind absorbs and openly responds to suggestion, if the rational *filters* of the mind are removed by creating conditions in which the conscious mind is relaxed, entranced or somnulent.

The human mind is made up of many levels of conditioning; influences from the past. Our present action arises from this bank of experiences. Hypnotic or suggestion techniques first create conditions in which the conscious mind is relaxed and then they aim to address the subconcious directly. In this way conditioning influences which are stored in the subconcious as memories of past consciousness may be reinforced or negated.

Most people use only a tiny amount of their mind/body potential so when the subconcious is manipulated many extraordinary and even seemingly superhuman feats may be performed by the mind and body. Knowledge of these techniques will also clarify the methods used by many of the mundane but insidious repressive control mechanisms of our daily life, such as advertising and political propaganda.

Trance hypnosis of one person by another is a powerful tool and thus a potentially dangerous weapon which cannot be adequately described in cryptic form here but there are a few simple self hypnosis or auto suggestion techniques that may be tried now and are simple, safe and instructive.

AUTO SUGGESTION

The principles of suggestion operate in daily life and only gradually merge into the intensified techniques known as hypnosis. Weak impressions repeated over a period of time will have a cumulative effect equal to that of a concentrated short period

PRACTICAL EXPERIMENT 1 short term/physical

Grip hands tightly together and concentrate attention to the exclusion of all else on the idea that your hands are stuck together — — They cannot be pulled apart — a great force is holding them together — the harder we pull the tighter they will stick together— ——etc. etc. Almost before we know it the body obeys the suggestion and we experience the extraordinary feeling of complete inability to unclasp our hands.

Similar experiments with other actions will begin to demonstrate that it is possible to realise extraordinary powers over the physical body.

NOTE: DANGER OF HYPNOTISM IS OF CURING SYMTOMS RATHER THAN CAUSES. SYMPTOMS MAY BE FORCED TO DISAPPEAR (eg. pain) AND THEN THE TROUBLE MAY GET WORSE WITHOUT ANY INDICATIONS.

PRACTICAL EXPERIMENT 2. longer term/mental.

Suggestions directed at changing mental mores should be given definite form by being put in writing. Suppose a person decides to take the most vulnerable point of his personality and strengthen it. He suffers from uncontrollable tantrums. He might take a sheet of paper and boldly write three suggestions
    1. I will have complete control over my temper at all times.
    2. I am always of good temper and self controlled
    3. Nothing can disturb me or make me angry.

Then at least three times a day or as often as is convenient he must vigourously reinforce these suggestions in his mind. Thinking them and fixing them upon the visual memory also saying them aloud so as to reach the brain through the auditory channel. The excercise takes only a few minutes but concentration must be great enough to give the idea Living Existence.
Mere repetition is a waste of time.

Effects should be noticeable after about a week. Suggestions can then be modified to suite the changed conditions.
This sounds rather like 'bluffing' yet its justification lies in the fact that the 'bluff' turns to truth.

PRACTICAL EXPERIMENT 3. Health.

By similar means the health may be improved through increased physical control. Complaints such as constipation and insomnia may be cured by auto suggestion. It often facilitates the fixing of a suggestion to ally it with some simple ritual. For example: to cure insomnia, as well as the repeated verbal suggestions a cup of warm milk may be taken before retiring, with each sip say with strong concentration. This milk is helping me to sleep —— I shall sleep soundly— —— I cannot keep awake ——— z z z z ...

this information is mainly from a book called
A Manual of HYPNOTISM by H. Ernest Hunt.
published by William Rider and Sons 1920.

HYPNOSIS

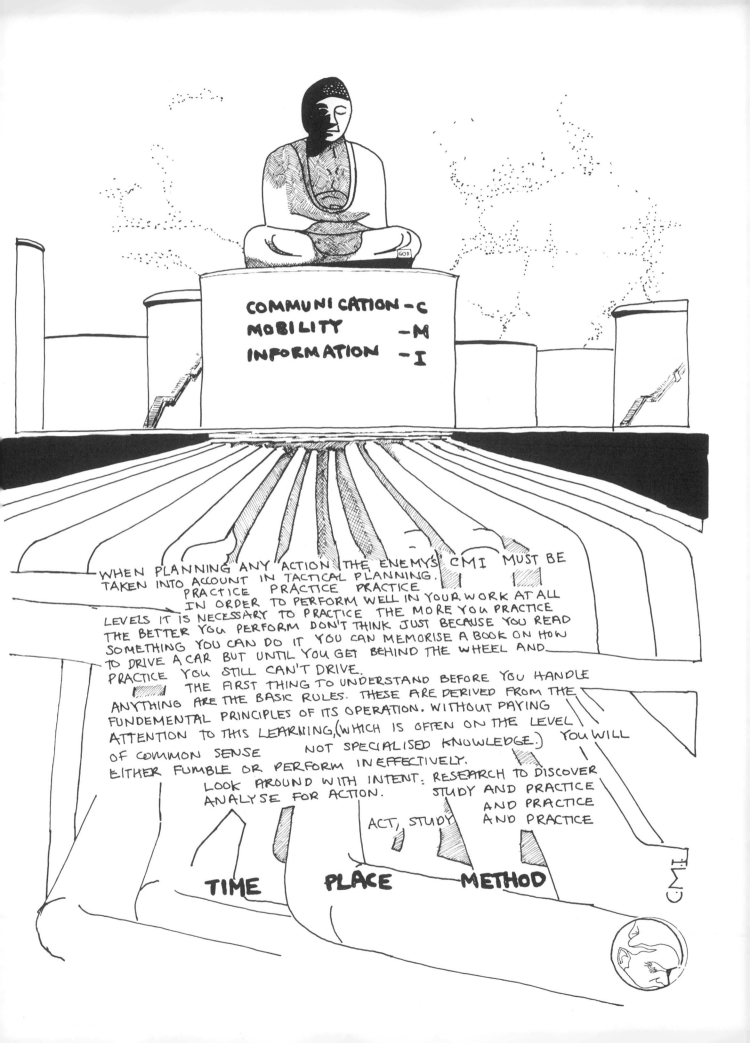

The Colonel issues BEGINNERS D.E.::::::::::::

"D.E. is a way of <u>doing</u>. It's a way of doing
everything you do. D.E. simply means doing
whatever you do in the <u>easiest</u> most relaxed
way you can manage, which is also the quickest and most efficient way as you will find
as you advance in D.E......"

You can start right now tidying up your flat,
moving furniture or books, washing dishes,
making tea, sorting papers. Consider the
weight of objects, exactly how much force is
needed to get the object from here to there.
Consider its shape and texture and function,
where exactly does it belong. Use just the
amount of force necessary to get the object
from here to there. Don't fumble grab jerk
an object. Drop cool possessive fingers on
it like a gentle old cop making a soft arr-
est. Guide a dust pan lightly to the floor
as if you were landing a plane. When you
touch an object, weigh it with your fingers,
feel your fingers on the object, the skin
blood muscles tendons of your hand and arm.
Consider these extensions of yourself as
precision instruments to perform every movement smoothly and well.

Handle objects with consideration and they
will show you all their little tricks. Don't
tug or pull at a zipper. Guide the little
metal teeth smoothly along feeling the sin-
uous ripples of cloth and flexible metal.
Replacing the cap on a tube of toothpaste ..
...(and this should be done at once always-
few things are worse than an uncapped tube
maladroitly squeezed twisting up out of the
bathroom glass drooling paste unless it be
a tube with a cap barbarously forced on all
askew against the threads)................
Replacing the cap let the very tips of your
fingers protrude beyond the cap contacting
the end of the tube guiding the cap into
place. Using your finger tips as a landing
gear will enable you to drop any light object silently and surely into its place.

Remember every object has its place. If you
don't find that place and put that thing there
it will jump out at you and trip you or rap
you painfully across the knuckles. It will
nudge you and clutch you and get in your
way. Often such objects belong in the
waste basket but often it's just that they
are out of place. Learn to place an object
firmly and quietly in its place and do not
let your fingers move that object as they
leave it there. When you put down a cup,
separate your fingers cleanly from the cup
...Do not let them catch in the handle and
if they do repeat movement until fingers
separate cleanly.

If you don't catch that nervous finger
that won't let go of that handle you may
twitch hot tea across the Duchess.

Never let a poorly executed sequence pass.
If you throw a match at a waste basket and
miss get right up and put that match in the
waste basket. If you have time repeat the
cast that failed. There is always a reason
for missing easy tosses. Repeat them and you
will find it.

If you rap your knuckles against a window
jamb or door, if you brush your leg against
a bed or desk, if you catch your foot in the
curled up corner of a rug, or strike a toe
against a desk or chair go back and repeat
the sequence.

You will find yourself surprised how far off
course you were to hit that window jamb,
that door, that chair. Get back on course
and do it again. How can you pilot a space
craft if you can't find your way round your
own apartment?

It's just like retaking a movie shot until you get
it right. And you will begin to feel yourself in
a movie, moving with ease and speed. But don't try
for speed at first. Try for relaxed smoothness taking
as much time as you need for performing the action. If
you drop an object, break an object, spill anything,
knock painfully against anything, galvanically clutch
an object, pay particular attention to retake. You
may find out why and forestall repeat performance. If
the object is broken sweep up pieces and remove from
the room at once. If object is intact or you have
duplicate object, repeat sequence. You may experience
a strange feeling as if the objects are alive and hos-
tile trying to twist out of your fingers, slam noisily
down on a table, jump out at you and stub your toe and
trip you. Repeat sequence until objects are brought to
order. Here is a student at work. At two feet he
tosses red plastic milk cap at the orange garbage bucket. The cap sails over the bucket like a flying saucer.
He tries again. Same result. He examines the cap and
finds that one edge is crushed down. He prises the
edge back into shape. Now the cap will drop obediently
into the bucket. Every object you touch is alive with
your life and your will.

The student tosses cigarette box at waste basket, and
it bounces out from the cardboard cover from a metal
coathanger which is resting diagonally across the waste
basket and never should be there at all. If an ash tray
is emptied into that waste basket the cardboard triangle
will split the ashes and the butts scattering both on
the floor. Student takes a box of matches from his coat
pocket preparatory to lighting cigarette from new package on table. With the matches in one hand he makes
another toss and misses of course his fingers are in
future time lighting a cigarette. He retrieves package
puts the matches down and now stooping slightly legs
bent hop skip over the washstand and into the waste
basket, miracle of the zen master who hits a target in
the dark these little miracles will occur more and more
often as you advance in DE.....the ball of paper tossed
over the shoulder into the waste basket, the blanket
flipped and settled just into place that seems to fold
itself under the brown satin fingers of an old Persian
merchant. Objects move into place at your lightest
touch. You slip into it like a film moving with such
ease that you hardly know that you are doing it. You
come into the kitchen expecting to find a sink full of
dirty dishes and instead every dish is put away and
the kitchen shines.

The student considers heavy objects. Tape recorder
on the desk taking up too much space and he doesn't
use it very often. So put it under the wash stand.
Weigh it with the hands. First attempt the cord and
plug leaps across the desk like a frightened snake. He
bumps his back on the washstand putting the recorder
under it. Try again, lift with legs not back. He hits
the lamp. He looks at that lamp. It is a horrible dis-
jointed object the joints tightened with a cellophane
tape disconnected when not in use the cord leaps out and
wraps around his feet sometimes jerking the lamp across
the desk. Remove that lamp from the room and buy a new
one. Now try again lifting, pivoting shifting dropping
on the legs just so and right under the wash stand.

You will discover clumsy things you've been doing for
years until you think that is just the way things are...
..Here is an American student who for years has <u>clawed</u>
at the red cap on English milk bottles.....you see
American caps have a little tab and he has been looking
for that old tab all these years. Then one day in a
friend's kitchen he saw a cap depressed at the centre.

D.E.

Next morning in he tries it and the miracle occurs. Just the right pressure in the centre and he lifts the cap off with deft fingers, and replaces it. He does this several times in winder and in awe and well he might, him a college professor and very technical too, planarium worms learn quicker than that.....for years he has been putting on his socks after he puts on his pants so he has to roll up pants and pants and socks get clawed up together so why not put the socks on before the pants? He is learning the simple miracles.

The Miracle of the Wash Stand Glass.....We all know the glass there on a rusty razor blade streaked with pink toothpaste a decapitated tube writhing up out of it.... quick fingers go to work on it and the Glass sparkles like the Holy Grail in the morning sunlight.

Now he does the wallet drill. For years he has carried his money in his left hand pocket of his pants reaching down to fish out the naked money, bumping his fingers against the edges of the sharp notes. Often the notes were in two stacks and pulling out the one could drop the other on the floor. The left side pocket of the pants is the most difficult to pick but worse things can happen than a picked pocket. One can dine out on that for a season.

Two manicured fingers sliding into the well-cut suit wafted into the waiting hand an engraved message from the Queen. Surely this is the easy way. Besides no student of DE would have his pocket picked applying DE in the street, picking his route in the crowds through slow walkers, don't get stuck behind that baby carriage, careful when you round a corner don't bump into somebody coming round the other way. When speed is crucial to the operation you must find your speed, the fastest you can perform the operation without error.

Don't try for speed at first it will come his fingers will rustle through the wallet with a touch light as dead leaves and crinkle discretely the note that will bribe a South American customs official into overlooking a shrunken head. The customs agent smiles a collector's smile, the smile of a connoisseur. Such a crinkle he has not heard since a French jewel thief with crudely forged papers made a crinkly sound over them with his hands and there is the note neatly folded in a false passport.

Now someone will say....."But if I have to think about every move I make.....?" You have only to think and break down movement into a series of still pictures to be studied and corrected because you have not found the easy way. Once you find the easy way you don't have to think about it. It will almost do itself.

Operations performed on yourself.....brushing teeth, washing etcetera can lead you to detect a defect before it develops. Here is a student with a light case of bleeding gums. His dentist has instructed him to massage gums by placing little splinters of wood called Interdens between the teeth and massaging gum with a see-saw motion. He snatches an Interden, opens his mouth in a stiff grimace, and jabs at the gum with a shaking hand. Now he remembers his DE. Start over. Take out the little splinters of wood like small chop sticks joined at the base and separate them gently. Now find where the bleeding is. Relax face and move Interden up and down gently firmly gum relaxed direct your attention to that spot. No not getting better and better just let the attention of your whole body flow there and all the healing power of your body flow with it. Everyday tasks become painful and boring because you think of it as WORK something solid and heavy to be fumbled and stumbled over. Overcome this block and you will find that DE can be applied to anything you do even the final discipline of doing nothing. The easier you do it the less you have to do. He who has learned to do nothing with his whole mind and body will have everything done for him.

D.E.!

Let us now apply DE to a simple test: The old Western quick draw gunfight. Only one gunfighter really grasped the principle of DE and that one was Wyatt Earp. Wyatt Earp said: "It's not the first shot that counts it's the first shot that hits. Point is to draw aim and fire and deliver the slug one inch above the belt buckle." That's DE. How fast can you do it and get it done? It is related that a young boy once incurred the wrath of Two Gun McGee. McGee has sworn to kill him and even now is preparing himself in a series of saloons. The boy has never been in a gunfight and Wyatt Earp advises him to leave town, while McGee is still two saloons away The boy refuses to leave.

"All right," Earp tells him. "You can hit a circle four inches square at six feet can't you? Alright, take your aim and hit it." Wyatt flattens himself against a wall calling out once more: "Take your time, kid." (How fast can you take your time, kid?) At this moment McGee bursts through the door a .45 in each hand spitting lead all over town. A drummer from St. Louis is a bit slow hitting the floor and catches a slug in the forehead. A boy peacefully eating chop suey in the Chinese Restaurant Huey Long next door stops a slug in the thigh. Now the kid draws his gun steadies it in both hands and fires at six feet hitting Two Gun McGee squarely in the stomach. The heavy slug knocks him back against the wall. He manages to get off one more shot and bring down the chandelier. The boy fires again and sends a bullet ripping through McGee's chest.

The beginner can think of DE as a game. You are running an obstacle course the obstacles set up by your opponent. As soon as you attempt to put DE into practice you will find that you have an opponent very clever and persistent and resourceful with detailed knowledge of your weaknesses and above all expert in diverting your attention for the moment necessary to drop a plate on the kitchen floor. Who or what is this opponent who makes you spill drop and fumble slip and fall?

Groddech and Freud called it the IT, a built-in self-destrctive mechanism. Mr. Hubbard calls it the Reactive Mind. You will disconnect it as you advance in DE. DE brings you into direct conflict with the IT in present time where you can control it with your moves. You can beat the IT in present time.

Take the inverse skill of the IT back into your own hands. These skills belong to you. Make them yours. You know where the wastebasket is. You can land an object in the waste basket over your shoulder. You know how to touch and move and pick up things. Regaining these physical skills is of course simply a prelude to regaining other skills and other knowledge that you have but can not make available for your use. You know your entire past history just what year month day and hour everything happened. If you have heard a language for any length of time you know that language. You have a computer in your brain. DE will show you how to use it, but that's another chapter.

DE applies to ALL operations carried out inside the body.....brain waves, digestion, blood pressure, and heart beat rate.....And that's another chapter....."And now I have stray cats to feed and my class at the Leprosarium, Lady Sutton-Smith raises a distant umbrella...
....
I hope you find your way............the address in empty streets....."

(This essay by Wm. Burroughs was first published in MAYFAIR. It is collected with other pieces in EXTERMINATOR CALDER & BOYARS/RICHARD SEAVER.)

Steam Tricycle (1899)

Live in a small well insulated home, shower using a watering can, cook in the oven or pressure cooker, do away with 'incidental lighting', wear long johns and a hat in winter use hand tools, keep fit digging the garden, mediate with the outside world by means of micro-electronics, find enjoy- -ment in the natural world rather than searching for satisfaction in the consumers costly quotidien.................. and then you won't need much energy. Simple more efficient and direct methods of keeping our life activity running smoothly preclude the necessity for large quantities of energy, (which are difficult to obtain from small home-run units) without suffering the   qualitative loss, that often acc- -ompanies the quantative   gain, of larger scale more distant processes that are not   in the direct control of the users.

solo electric

for details — Halkin Propulsions Suite 8, 25 Jermyn St. LONDON. SW1 01 437 4534

EFFICIENCY

IDEA GENERATOR

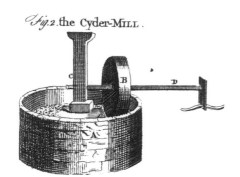

IMPROVED HORSE AND CATTLE GEARS.

Fig.2. the Cyder-MILL.

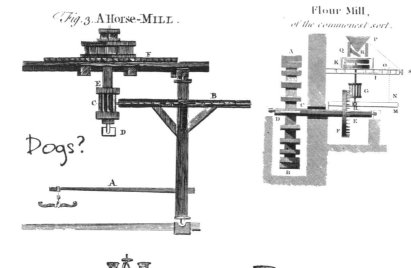

Fig.3. A Horse-MILL.

Flour Mill,
of the commonest sort.

Dogs?

STEAM FLOUR MILL.   BEAN MILL.

The extremely versatile
CARALITE converts to
a handlamp simply by
using battery frame No.
86014 which costs only
8/6.

Microwave ovens
*Dysona Industries Ltd., Molly Millars
Lane, Wokingham, Berks.*
The first three Dysona microwave ovens,
all of 1·15kW output, but with differing
timing devices, are claimed to be in
advance of all competitive products and
capable of totally eliminating food waste
in industrial and commercial restaurants.
They employ very high frequency radio
waves to heat the inside of food and work
15 times faster than conventional cookers
at one-sixth of their fuel costs The 'time
key' model, operated by small plastic
keys to match meal heating times, and
specially designed for use with auto-
mated meal vending machines, costs
£425 and is claimed to represent a saving
of £200 on the imported machine which
is the only alternative. Cooking speeds
are extremely rapid. A 9lb chicken can be
microwave cooked in 10 minutes—at a
fuel cost of less than a penny—and
sponge cakes and batter puddings take
two minutes.

LATE ADDITIONS

Starting out as an "extension of man", technology is transformed into
a force above man, orchestrating his life according to a score contrived
by an industrial bureaucracy; not *men*, I repeat, but *bureaucracies*, i.e.,
social machines.   With the arrival of the fully automatic machine as
the predominant means of production, man becomes an extension of
the machine, not only of mechanical devices in the productive process
but also of social devices in the social process.   Man ceases to exist in
almost any respect for his own sake.   Society is ruled by the harsh
maxim: production for the sake of production.   The decline from
craftsman to worker, from the active to the increasingly passive
personality, is completed by man *qua* consumer—an economic entity
whose tastes, values, thoughts, and sensibilities are engineered by
bureaucratic 'teams' in 'think tanks'.   Man, standardized by machines,
is finally reduced to a machine.

from <u>Towards a Liberatory Technology</u>. Lewis Herber. Anarchy. no.78 . 1967.

MAP SECTION

North America maps symbolise next scale step down view after global patterns. British map takes you another stage further in.

The use of national or state charts, maps, facts and figures are limited in that any particular locality is likely to show considerable variance within its overall mean. (generalisations.) So, the following pages only tell one side of the story; the other side must be told by you for your own locality. No need for complex ~~measuring equipment before you~~ start (you can feel the wind on your face) .... on the spot research. Gear for finer measurements may be borrowed from the local college, meteorological station etc.
Monitor your neighbourhood pulse and fabric. Let your neighbours know about the resources they ~~have~~ right there.

HOURS OF SUNSHINE
PER YEAR

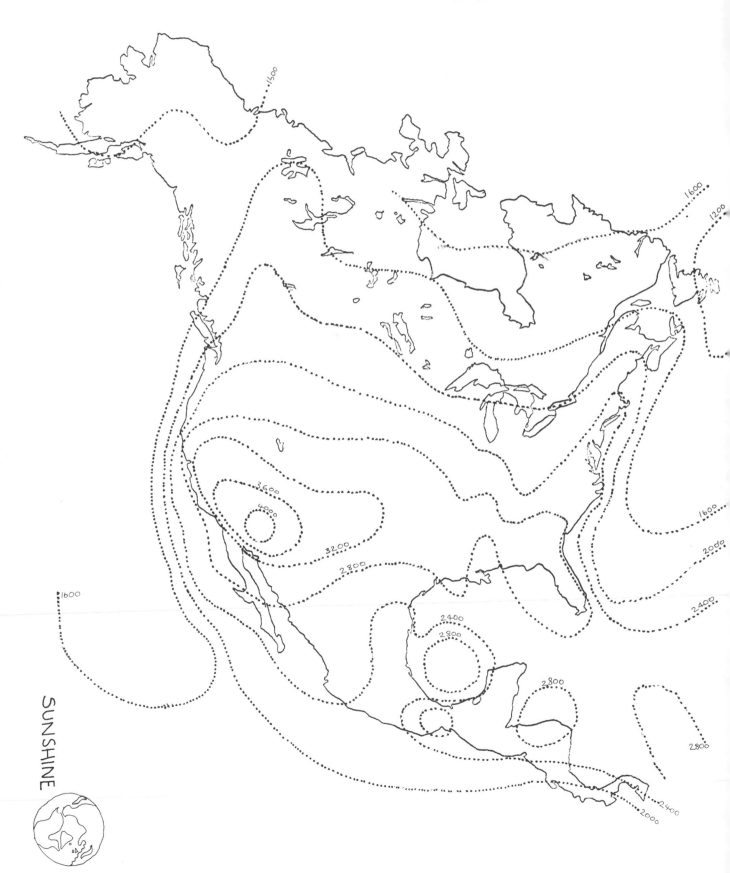

SUNSHINE

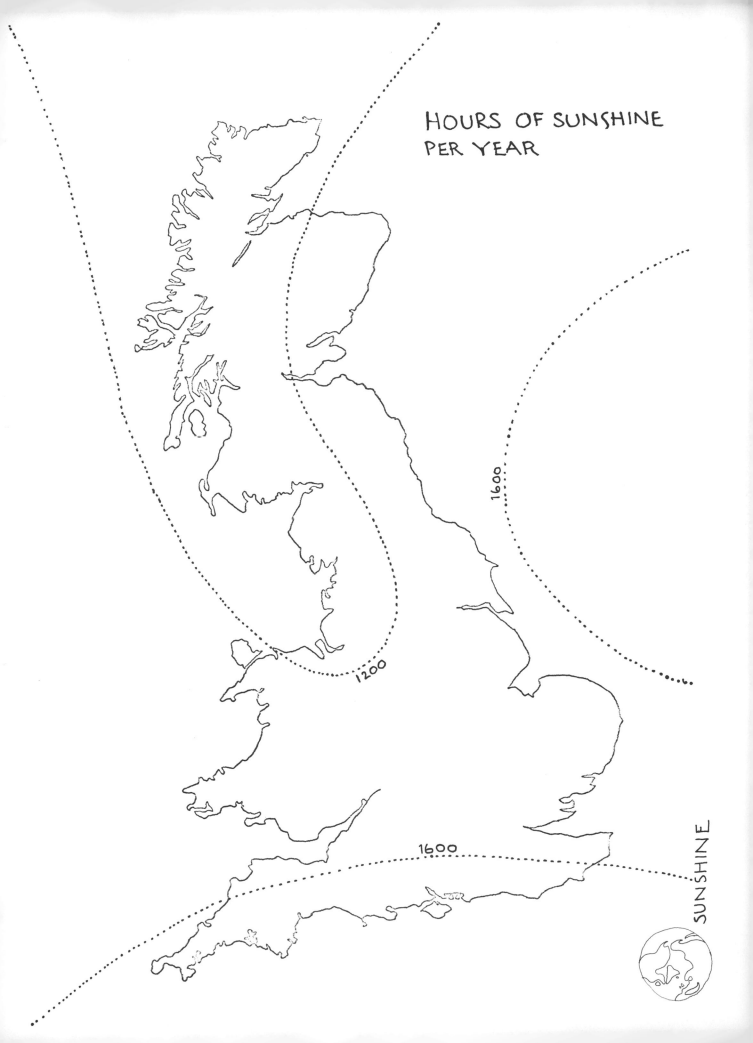

HOURS OF SUNSHINE
PER YEAR

1600

1200

1600

SUNSHINE

WIND SPEED
(WINTER)

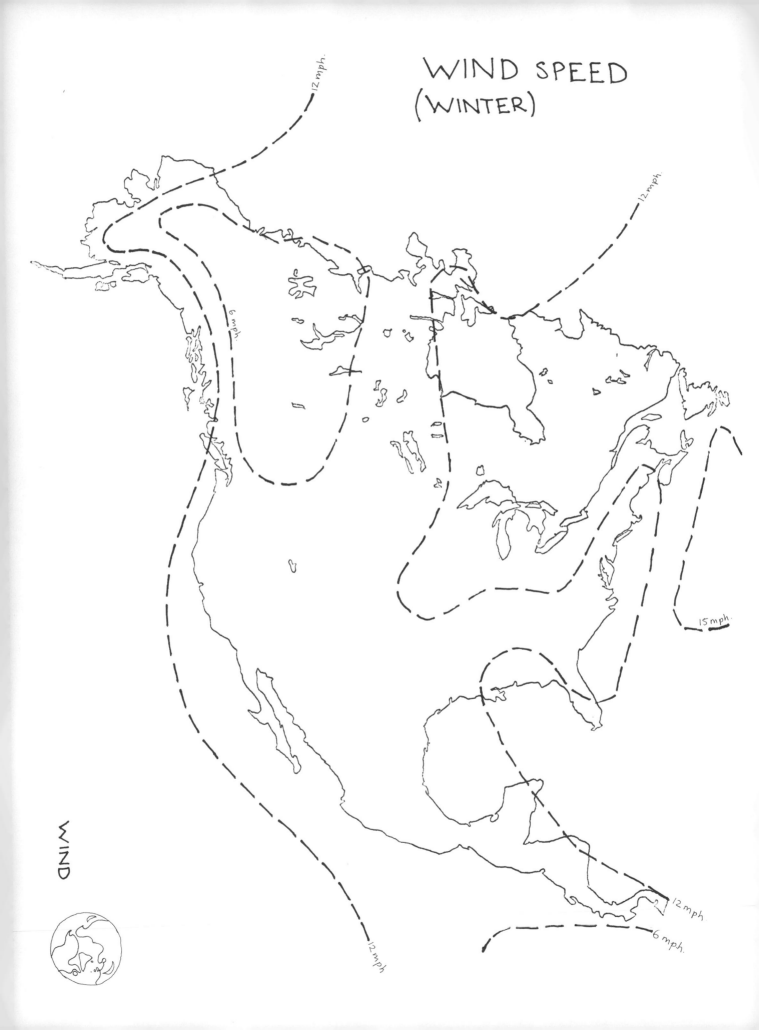

12 mph.

12 mph.

6 mph.

15 mph.

WIND

12 mph

12 mph.

6 mph.

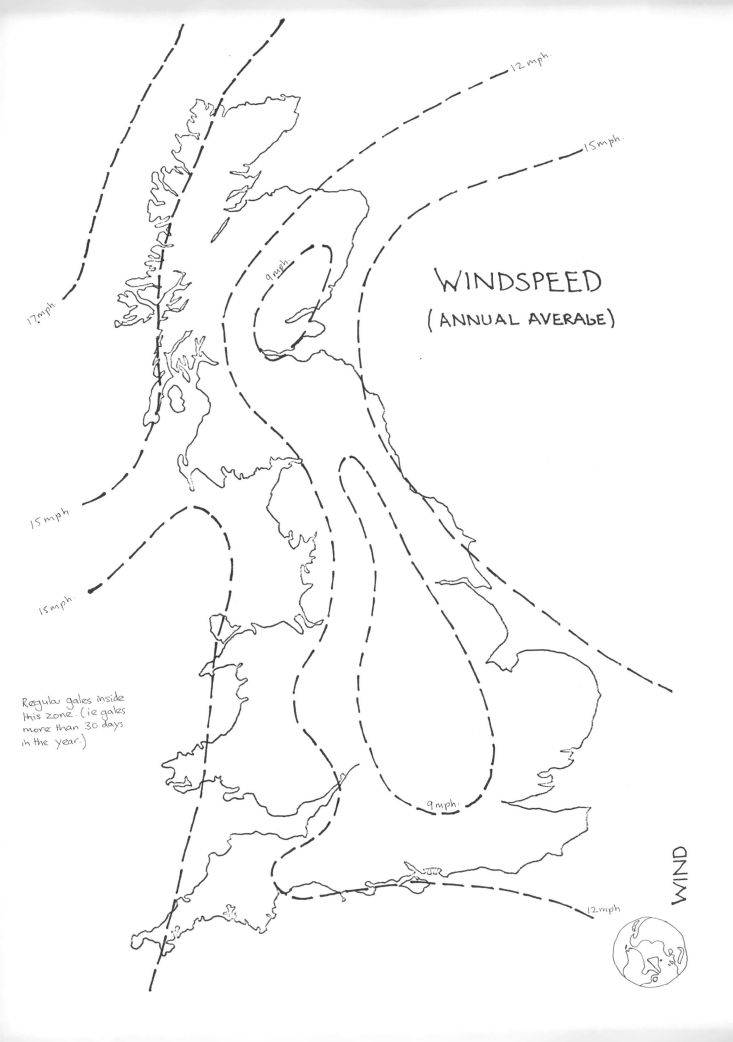

WINDSPEED
(ANNUAL AVERAGE)

17 mph.

12 mph.

15 mph.

9 mph.

15 mph.

15 mph.

Regular gales inside
this zone. (ie gales
more than 30 days
in the year.)

9 mph.

9 mph.

12 mph.

WIND

WATER
(RIVERS AND TIDE)

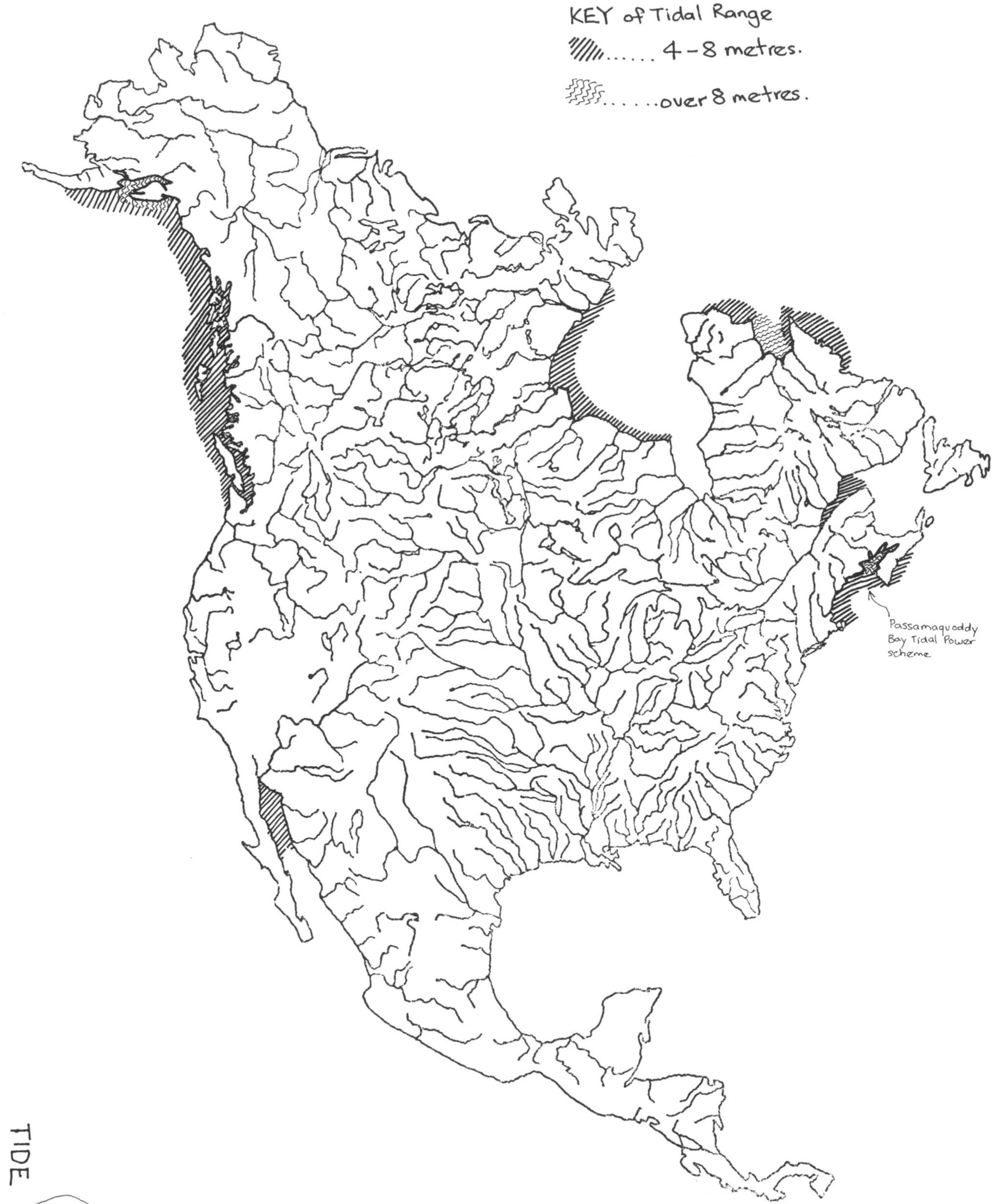

KEY of Tidal Range

///...... 4 – 8 metres.

≋≋......over 8 metres.

Passamaquoddy
Bay Tidal Power
scheme

TIDE

WATER
(RIVERS AND TIDE)

N.B. NUMBERS AROUND COAST
INDICATE TIDAL RANGE IN YARDS.

WATER

HOT SPRINGS

Source: Thermal Springs pp. 105-125 PLACE vol. 1. no. 2. Star Route 1. 1972.

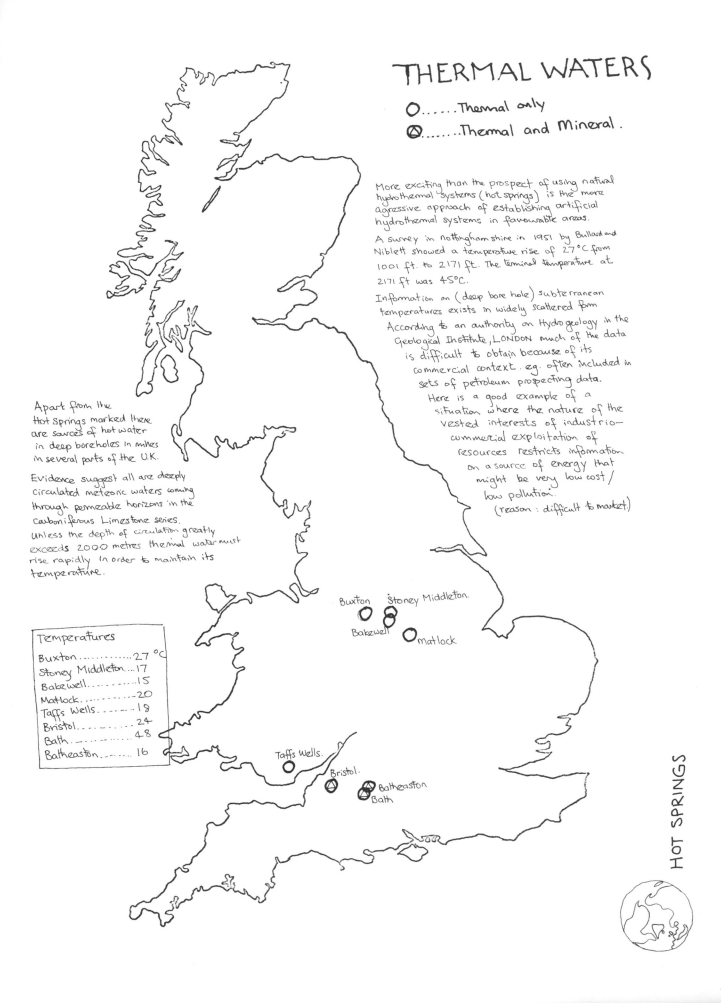

THERMAL WATERS

O......Thermal only

⊕........Thermal and Mineral.

More exciting than the prospect of using natural hydrothermal systems (hot springs) is the more aggressive approach of establishing artificial hydrothermal systems in favourable areas.

A survey in Nottinghamshire in 1951 by Bullard and Niblett showed a temperature rise of 27°C from 1001 ft. to 2171 ft. The terminal temperature at 2171 ft was 45°C.

Information on (deep bore hole) subterranean temperatures exists in widely scattered form

According to an authority on Hydrogeology in the Geological Institute, LONDON much of the data is difficult to obtain because of its commercial context. eg. often included in sets of petroleum prospecting data.

Here is a good example of a situation where the nature of the vested interests of industrio-commercial exploitation of resources restricts information on a source of energy that might be very low cost / low pollution.

(reason : difficult to market.)

Apart from the Hot Springs marked there are sources of hot water in deep boreholes in mines in several parts of the U.K.

Evidence suggest all are deeply circulated meteoric waters coming through permeable horizons in the Carboniferous Limestone series. Unless the depth of circulation greatly exceeds 2000 metres thermal water must rise rapidly in order to maintain its temperature.

Buxton   Stoney Middleton.

Bakewell   Matlock

Temperatures
Buxton.............27 °C
Stoney Middleton....17
Bakewell...........15
Matlock............20
Taffs Wells........18
Bristol............24
Bath...............48
Batheaston........16

Taffs Wells.

Bristol.

Batheaston

Bath

HOT SPRINGS

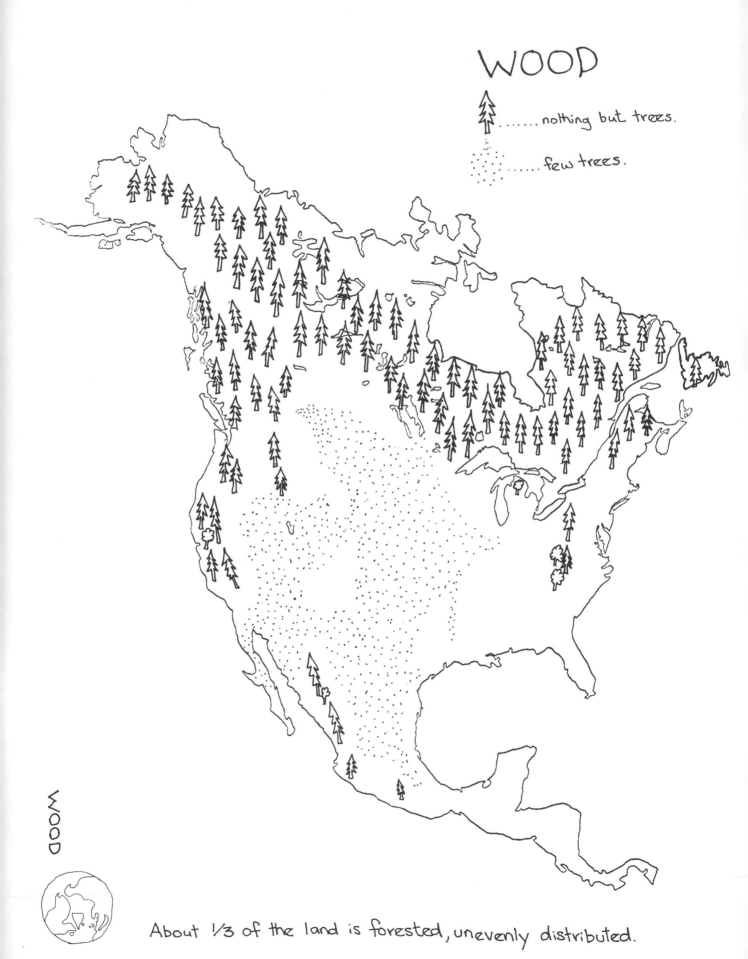

WOOD

.... nothing but trees.

.... few trees.

WOOD

About 1/3 of the land is forested, unevenly distributed.

WOODs

WOOD

FOSSIL RESOURCES

||||| ..... COAL

≡≡≡ ..... OIL

/// ..... GAS

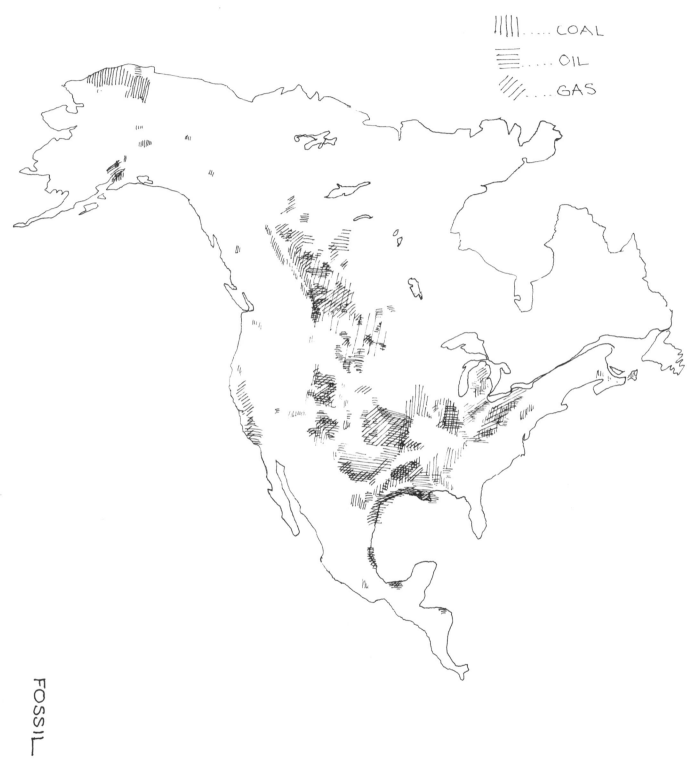

FOSSIL

FOSSIL

OIL

NATURAL
GAS

FOSSIL

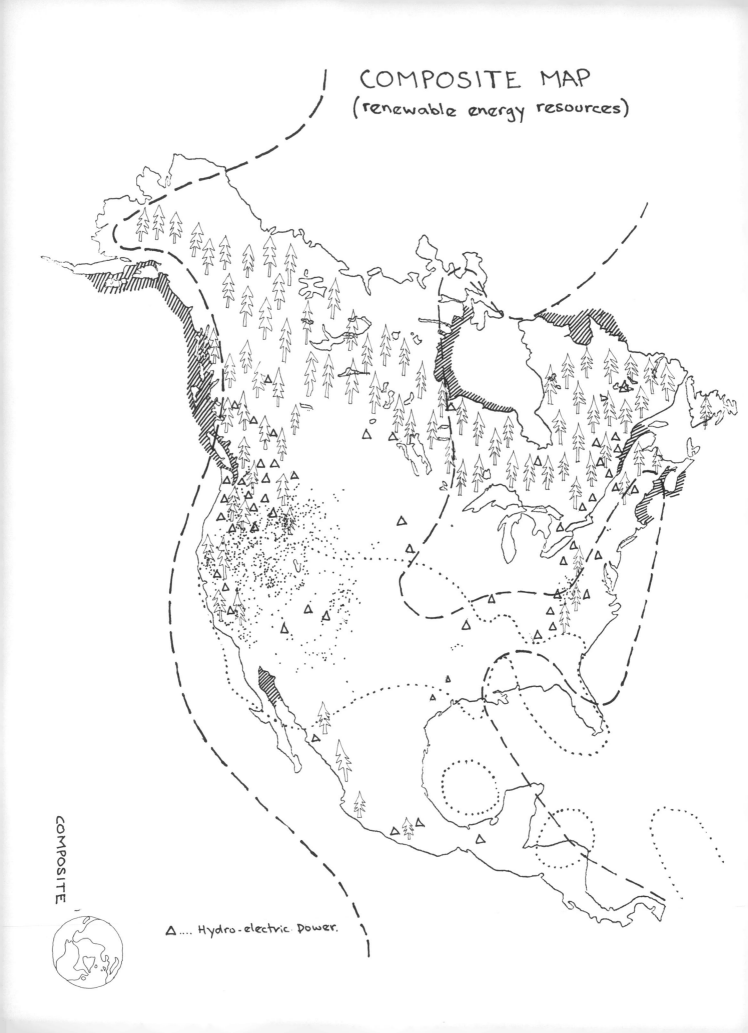

COMPOSITE MAP
(renewable energy resources)

COMPOSITE

△ .... Hydro-electric power.

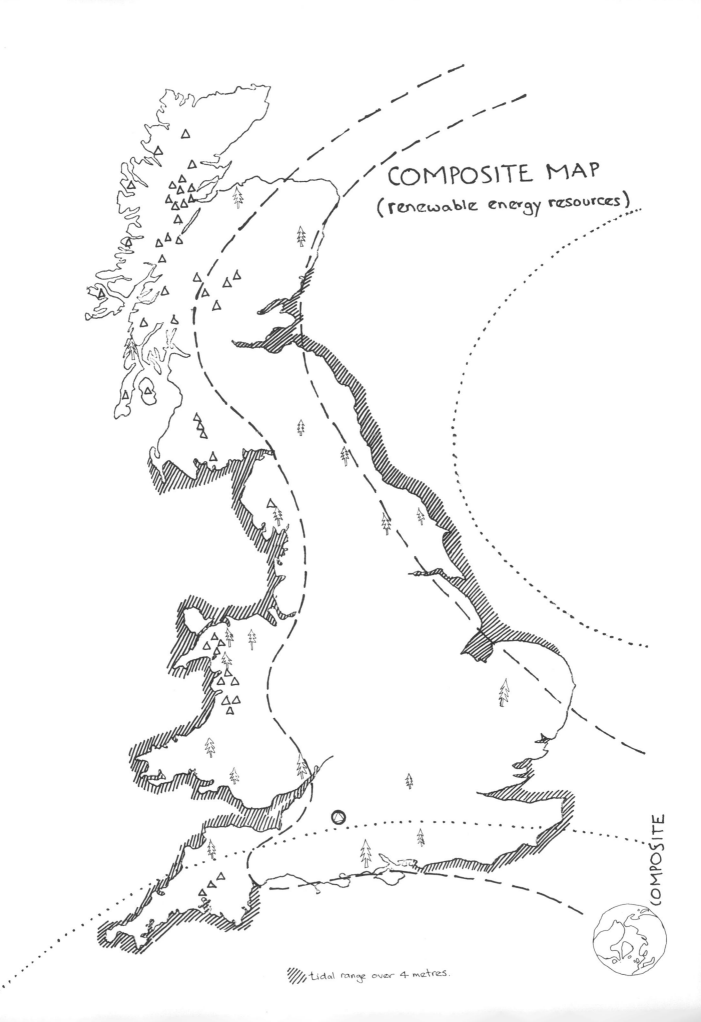

COMPOSITE MAP
(renewable energy resources)

COMPOSITE

////// tidal range over 4 metres.

CONCLUDING NOTES.   RE composite map Britain ⟶
areas with rich ___ewa___ energy resources are
often DEPOPULATING and that **u**_____**n** festers
in areas that have LEAST RENEWABLE **E**____**y**
Also notice ⟶ the 'NEW' sources of
energy compliment the old ones. It seems
to suggest that a ___**1AT**___ evenly dispersed
would have FEW resource problems IF they
relied on what was LOCALLY AVAILABLE relying
on what is LOCALLY AVAILABLE means
greater possibility of **CONTROL** by the __**e**__
who USE the RESOURCES + ___**bil**___ of
supply. Stability of ____**y**   +DECENTRALISED
power (armed) means PEACE   (reduced scale of
conflict) but this SITUATION could not
BE accepted by the elite group of people
who have   in vested in terests in the PRESENT
arrangement (top of the hierachy ⟶
__**ss**___) They will use (aready have)
__**Lic**_ + _**rm**_ + _**ed**__ to try
to stop any ACTION that could lead
in this direction (Workers Power through
__**n**_**e**__ _**t**__**k**_) Meet one crude
force with another ⟶ bloody risky   +
'new' state with old characteristics (SEPARATION)
what IS necessary is GRASSROOT
_____**sat**___ eg street action committee
NETWORKS RICHLY INFORMED ready for
___**truc**___ + CREATION. JOIN
TO-GETHER.

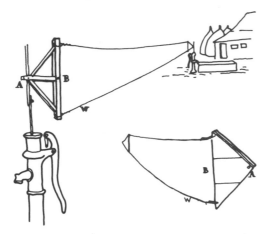

TRANSMISSION OF WINDMILL ENERGY

"Sometimes our farmers find the well so situated that the windmill and tower cannot be set up without interfering with the porch, kitchen, and milkhouse; in which event, a walking beam, or rocker shaft often connects the mill and pump. If too distant, recourse is had to the angle block and connecting wires. In this way the mill at the house can be geared to run the pump at the barn, or even in a neighboring field.

The better way is to purchase such things of the man whose business it is to make them, and so have undivided time for one's own business. But when one wishes to make his own angles it is a simple matter, and several sketches are appended to suggest what may be done in transmitting the energy of the mill by means of two oscillating wires and a couple of quadrants cut out of a board."

A attachment to pump rod.
B attachment to tower or stationary support.
W strong fencing wire.

The Homemade Windmills of Nebraska

BIBLIOGRAPHY

INTRODUCTORY. These books are general reference on Energy.

✳ALTERNATIVE SOURCES OF ENERGY (magazine)
      Don Marier, ed.
      Route 1, Box 36B
      Minong, Wisconsin, U.S.54859
      (issue 9 is a comprehensive U.S. orientated
      bibliography.)

COMMUNITIES AND ECOSYSTEMS
      R.H.Whittaker
      Holt, Rinehart & Winston, 1963

✳ DESIGNING FOR SURVIVAL
      C. Moorcraft
      A.D. Magazine, 7, 1972.

DESIGN WITH CLIMATE
      Victor Olgyay
      Princeton, 1972

✳ THE ECOL OPERATION: ECOLOGY + BUILDING + COMMON SENSE
      Alvaro Ortega, et al.
      School of Architecture, McGill University, Montreal.
      (Minimum cost housing studies, $3.50)

ENERGY
      Scientific American Magazine
      Sept. 1971
      (Avalable as a Scientific American Offprint)

ENERGY CONSUMPTION AND PER CAPITA STATISTICS
      United Nations Statistical Year Book

ENERGY EXCHANGE IN THE BIOSPHERE
      D.M.Gates
      Harper and Row, 1962

ENERGY IN THE FUTURE
      P.C.Putnam
      Van Nostrand, 1953

ENERGY INTO POWER
      E.G.Sterland
      Aldous, 1957

ENVIRONMENT, POWER AND SOCIETY
      H.T.Odum
      Wiley-Interscience, 1971

FUEL POLICY
      H.M.S.O., London, 1967

GEOGRAPHY OF ENERGY, The
      G.Manners
      Hutchinson, London, 1965

HISTORY OF TECHNOLOGY, The
      C.Singer, ed.
      Oxford University Press, 1958

INTERNATIONAL PETROLEUM ENCYCLOPAEDIA
      Petroleum Publishing, 1969

MAN AND ENERGY
      A.R.Ubbelohde
      Hutchinson, 1954
      (also available in Pelican)

MOTHER EARTH NEWS
      P.O.Box 38
      Madison, Ohio
      U.S.44057
      (A Magazine)

NATURAL SOURCES OF POWER
      R.S.Ball
      Constable, London, 1908

✳ NEW SOURCES OF ENERGY, Vols. 1-7.
      United Nations, 1964
      Vol.1, General. Vol.2 & 3, Geothermal.
      Vols. 4,5,&6 Solar. Vol.7, Wind.

✳ indicates recommended reference.

INTRODUCTORY BIBLIOGRAPHY (Cont.)

OIL AND WORLD POWER
    P.R.Odell
    Pelican, 1970

QUEST FOR POWER, The
    Vowles
    Chapman & Hall, London, 1931

SOME REFERENCES TO THE MENACE OF NUCLEAR FISSION
    J.R.J.Bond
    36, Hammond Road
    Southall, Middlesex
    England

TECHNOLOGY IN THE ANCIENT WORLD
    H. Hodges
    Penguin, 1971

TOWARDS A LIBERATORY TECHNOLOGY
    Lewis Herber
    Anarchy, 78, August 1967
    (Magazine)

✱ UNDERCURRENTS
    34, Chomley Gardens
    Aldred Road
    London, N.W.6., England
    (Magazine)

SOLAR POWER BIBLIOGRAPHY

ALGAE, MAN AND THE ENVIRONMENT
    D.F.Jackson (ed.)
    Syracuse University Press, 1968

COMING AGE OF SOLAR ENERGY
    Halacy
    Harper & Row   1966

CONVERSION OF SOLAR ENERGY TO ELECTRICITY
VIA ALGAE GROWTH
    W.J.Oswald & H.B.Gotass
    Transactions of Amer. Soc. of Civil Engineers
    1957

DIRECT ENERGY CONVERSION
    Angrist
    (Pub. unknown) 1971

✱ DIRECT USE OF THE SUN'S ENERGY
    F.Daniels
    Yale, 1970

HOME GENERATION OF POWER BY PHOTOVOLTANIC
    CONVERSION OF SOLAR ENERGY
    J.F.Elliot
    Electrical Engineering, Sept. 1960

HOW TO USE THE SUN AROUND THE HOME
    J.Belanger
    Organic Gardening Magazine, Jan. 72.

INTRODUCTION TO THE UTILIZATION OF SOLAR ENERGY
    Zarem & Erway, eds.
    McGraw Hill, 1963

MASS CULTIVATION OF ALGAE
    H.Tamiya
    Annual Review of Plant Physiology, 8, 1957

POSSIBILITIES FOR THE UTILIZATION OF SOLAR ENERGY
    IN UNDERDEVELOPED AREAS
    G.T.Ward
    F.A.O., Informal working bulletin, Land &
    Water Division

PROCEEDINGS OF WORLD SYMPOSIUM OF APPLIED
    SOLAR ENERGY (1955)
    Stanford Research Inst., Phoenix, Ariz., 1956

SOLAR ENERGY BIBLIOGRAPHY (Cont.)

SOLAR AND AEOLIAN ENERGY
    A.G.Spanides, ed.
    Plenum, 1964

SOLAR DISTILLATION
    United Nations, 1970
    Sales Number E.70.11.B1.

SOLAR ENERGY
    H.Ran
    Macmillan, 1964

SOLAR ENERGY (Periodical)
    Solar Energy Society
    Arizona State University
    Tempe, Arizona

SOLAR ENERGY RESEARCH
    F.Daniels and J.A.Duffie, eds.
    Thames & Hudson, London, 1955

SOLAR ENERGY FOR MAN
    B.J.Brinkworth
    Compton, 1972

✱ SOLAR ENERGY IN HOUSING
    C.Moorcraft
    Architectural Design Mag. 10, 1973

SOLAR RADIATION
    N.Robinson
    Elsevier (Amsterdam) 1966

✱ SOLAR WATER HEATING IN SOUTH AFRICA
    D.Chinnery
    National Building Research Institute
    Bulletin 44, C.S.I.R. Research Report 248
    Pretoria, South Africa

THE SUN
    E.Caloy
    Prentice Hall.,1963

THE SUN MOTOR
    J.Ericsson
    Nature, Vol.29, p.217
    & Harpers Weekly, Vol.31, Jan 1887, p.10.

THE USE OF SOLAR AND SKY RADIATION FOR AIR COND-
    ITIONING OF PNEUMATIC STRUCTURES
    Proceedings of the 1st International
        Colloquium of Pneumatic Structures
    Stuttgart, 1967

YOUR SOLAR HOUSE
    M.J.Simon, ed.
    Simon & Shuster, New York 1947.

WIND BIBLIOGRAPHY

AERONAUTICAL RESEARCH COUNCIL PUBLICATIONS
    List Number 8
    H.M.S.O., London, yearly.

BRITISH WINDMILLS AND WATERMILLS
    C.P.Skilton
    Collins, London, 1947

COUNTRYMAN AT WORK, The
    Thomas Hennell
    Architectural Press, 1947

DRAINING OF THE FENS, The
    H.C.Darby
    Cambridge University Press, Cambridge, 1940.

DUTCH WINDMILL, The
    Frederick Storhuyzen
    Universe Books, New York, 1963
    & Merlin Press, 1962

BIBLIOGRAPHY 2.

WIND BIBLIOGRAPHY (Cont.)

THE EARTH'S ATMOSPHERE AS A SOURCE OF
    ELECTRIC POWER
    O.Jefimenko
    W.Virginia University Magazine, Spring 71
    also Am. Journal of Physics, Vol.39, No.7
    pp.776-778.

ELECTRIC POWER FROM THE WIND
    Percy H.Thomas
    U.S.Federal Power Commission, 1945

ENGLISH WINDMILL, The
    Rex Wailes
    Routledge, London, 1954

ENGLISH WINDMILLS, Vol.II
    Donald Smith
    Architectural Press, London, 1932
    (Mills in Buckinghamshire, Essex, Hertfordshire
        Middlesex and London)

EXPERIMENTAL ENQUIRY CONCERNING THE NATURAL POWERS
    OF WATER AND WIND TO TURN MILLS AND OTHER
    MACHINES, DEPENDING ON A CIRCULAR MOTION, An
    John Smeaton
    I.&J.Taylor, London, 1794

✷ GENERATION OF ELECTRICITY BY WIND POWER, The
    E.W.Golding
    Spon, 1955

HISTORY OF CORN MILLING
    Richard Bennett and John Elton
    Simpkin Marshall, 1898, 1899, 1900, & 1904
    4 Volumes, Volume II (Watermills and Windmills)
        particularly useful

HOMEMADE WINDMILLS OF NEBRASKA, The
    E.R.Barbour
    Bulletin 59
    U.S.Agricultural Experimental Station of
        Nebraska, 1897.

INFLUENCE OF SHELTERBELTS ON MICROCLIMATE, The
    J.M.Caborn
    Quarterly Journal of the Royal Meteorological
        Society, Number 81, pp.112-115.

INTRODUCTION TO THE THEORY OF FLOW MACHINES
    A.Betz
    Pergamon Press, 1966

KITES, AN HISTORICAL SURVEY
    C.Hart
    Faber

MEDIEVAL TECHNOLOGY AND SOCIAL CHANGE
    Lynn White, Jr.
    OUP, New York, 1962

OLD WATERMILLS AND WINDMILLS
    R.Thurston Hopkins
    Philip Allen

POWER FROM THE WIND
    P.C.Putnam
    Van Nostrand, 1948

S-ROTOR AND ITS APPLICATION, The
    S.J.Savonius
    Mechanical Engineering, Vol.53, No.5
        May, 1931

STORY OF THE ROTOR, The
    A.Flettnor
    Crosby Lockwood, 1926

THEORY OF WING SECTIONS
    I.H.Abbott & A.E.von Doenhoff
    Dover, New York, 1959

TRANSACTIONS OF THE SECOND SYMPOSIUM OF
    MOLINOLOGY
    Soc. for Protection of Ancient Buildings
    London, 1969. (£4.00)

WATERMILLS AND WINDMILLS
    R.Bennett and J.Elton
    E.P., London, 1973, repr. of 1899 ed.

WATERMILLS AND WINDMILLS
    William Coles Finch
    C.W.Daniel, 1933

WIND AND SOLAR ENERGY
    New Delhi Symposium
    UNESCO, 1954

WINDCRAFT THEORY AND PRACTICE
    K.Bilau
    Paul Parey, Berlin, 1927

WINDMILL AS A PRIME MOVER, The
    Wolff
    Wiley, New York, 1885

WINDMILLS AND MILLWRIGHTING
    S.W.Freese
    David & Charles, Newton Abbott, U.K., 1971

WINDMILLS AND WATERMILLS
    John Reynolds
    Hugh Evelyn, London, 1970

WINDMILLS & WINDMOTORS
    Model Engineer Series, No.36
    Percival Marshal & Co. (1920's?)

WINDMILLS FOR THE GENERATION OF ELECTRICITY
    Cameron Brown
    National Institute of Agricultural
        Engineering Library, May 1933
    9 different types.

WINDMILLS FOR LIFTING WATER AND GENERATING
    ELECTRICITY ON THE FARM
    E.W.Goldring
    F.A.O. Informal Working Bulletin 17.

WINDMILLS IN ENGLAND
    Rex Wailes
    Architectural Press, London, 1948

WINDMILLS IN SUSSEX
    Peter Hemming
    C.S.Daniel, 1936

WINDMILLS OF SURREY AND INNER LONDON, The
    K.G.Farries and M.T.Mason
    Charles Skilton, 1966

WIND ROTOR IN THEORY AND PRACTICE
    S.J.Savonius
    Savonius & Co., Helsingfors, Finland

WIND SURVEY OF THE UNITED KINGDOM
    H.M.S.O., London

YACHT RACING, THE AERODYNAMICS OF SAILS
    Manfred Curry
    G.Bell, London, 1949

WIND BIBLIOGRAPHY, PAMPHLETS

ELECTRICAL RESEARCH INSTITUTE LEAFLETS
    Of particular interest in the series:

    Tech.Report 1B/T4: Aerodynamics of
    Windmills Used for the Generation
    of Electricity
    Sterne & Rose

BIBLIOGRAPHY 3.

WIND BIBLIOGRAPHY, PAMPHLETS, Cont.

ELECTRICAL RESEARCH INSTITUTE LEAFLETS, Cont.
Tech.Report CT/122 (1960): The Automatic
Operation of a Medium Sized Wind
Driven Generator Running in Isolation
J.G.Walker
14pp.

Tech.Report CT/118: The Combination of Local
Energy Resources to Provide Power
Supplies in Underdeveloped Areas

Tech.Report CT/106 (1951): The Design and
Development of 3 New Types of Gust
Anemometer
H.H.Rosebrock
37pp

Tech.Report CT/114 (1956): An Experimental
Study of Wind Structure
M.P.Wax
24pp

Tech.Report 119 (1957): A Preliminary Report
on the Design and Performance of Ducted
Windmills
Lilley & Rainbird
65pp

Tech.Report CT/112 (1954): The Use of Wind
Power in Denmark
Golding & Stodhard

Tech.Report CT/115 (1957): Wind Data Related
to the Generation of Electricity by
Wind Power
J.R.Tagg
52pp

Tech.Report CT/120 (1958): Windmills for
Electricity Supply in Remote Areas
Gimpel & Stodhart
24pp

WIND BIBLIOGRAPHY, PAMPHLETS

BRACE RESEARCH INSTITUTE PAMPHLETS

MT 7: The Design, Development and Testing of
a Low Cost 10hp Windmill Prime Mover
R.E.Chilcott
July 1969

Do-It-Yourself Leaflet No.5: How to Construct
a Cheap Wind Machine for Pumping Water
A.Bodek
Feb. 1965

Notes on the Development of the BRACE Airscrew
Windmill as a Prime Mover
R.E.Chilcott
Leaflet M.21. Sept. 1967.

Performance Test of a Savonins Rotor
Tech.Report T.10. Jan.1964
Bodek & Simonds

Performance Test of an 8 Meter Andreau Windmill
Tech.Report No.12. Feb. 1964
A.Bodek

Wind-Electric Report
Diploma Report D4 August 1963
C. Sanchez-Wilar

BIBLIOGRAPHY 4.

FIRE BIBLIOGRAPHY

THE ART OF TRAVEL
Francis Galton
John Murray, London, many eds. to 1971

BRITISH RESEARCH STATION DIGEST NO. 16
British Research Station
Garston, Hertfordshire, U.K.

FUELS AND FIRING EQUIPMENT FOR NURSERIES
Ministry of Agriculture, HML4, 2½p.

GLASSHOUSE HEATING SYSTEMS
Ministry of Agriculture, 9p

GENGAS (Wood Gas)
Academy of Sciences of Swedish Engineering
Stockholm, 1950

HOME FIRES BURNING. The History of Domestic
Heating and Cooking, Lawrence Wright
Routledge, London, 1964

✳ THE OWNER BUILT HOME (fire & solar)
Ken Ken
Ken Ken Drafting
Sierra Route
Oakhurst, California
U.S.93644

SOLID FUEL INSTALLATIONS
Post-War Building Studies No.10, 1944
British Coal Utilization Research Assoc.

WOOD FIRES FOR THE COUNTRY HOUSE AND COTTAGE
William Robinson
John Murray, London

WOODLAND CRAFTS OF BRITAIN
Herbert L. Edin
Reprint of 1949 ed.
David & Charles, U.K., 1973

WOOD WASTES AS FUEL
No.41 Leaflet (A)
Forest Products Research Lab.
Ministry of Technology, 1956

METHANE BIBLIOGRAPHY

✳BIO-GAS PLANT
Ram Bux Singh
Gobar Gas Station, 1971
Ajitmal, Uttar Pradesh, India

CHARACTERISTICS AND TREATMENT OF WASTES FROM A
A CONFINEMENT HOG PRODUCTION UNIT
Eliseos Paul Taiganides
University Microfilms Inc., 1963
Ann Arbor, Michigan

✳ COMPOSTING
Monograph Series No.31
World Health Organization, 1956
by H.B.Gotaas

GAS PRODUCTION ON THE FARM
Lord Iveagh
Power Farmer 7, p.87, 1951

✳ METHANE DIGESTORS FOR FUEL GAS AND FERTILIZER
Richard Merril
New Alchemy Institute---West
15 W. Anapamu
Santa Barbara, California, U.S.93101.
(a practical book.)

METHANE BIBLIOGRAPHY, Cont.

✱ METHANE: FUEL OF THE FUTURE
    Bell, Boulter, Dunlop, & Keiller
    Singer, 1973. 75p
    (Not very practical; but extensive Bibliog.)

MICRO-ORGANISMS AS ALLIES
    C.L.Duddington
    Faber, 1961

THE PRODUCTION AND USE OF METHANE GAS ON THE FARM
    F.A.Skinner, C.A.Scarlett & C.N.Harvey
    Soil Microbiology Dept.
    Rothamstead Experimental Station
    Rothampstead, nr. Harpenden, Herts., U.K.
    Feb.1958

FARM METHANE PRODUCTION
    Part II of A Report on a Visit to Germany and
    Holland, April/May 1961.
    Mechanical Engineers' Dept.
    British Society for Research in Agricultural
        Engineering

RIVER POLLUTION (Vol.2)
    L.Klein
    Butterworth, 1962

SEWERAGE AND SEWAGE TREATMENT
    H.E.BABBIT & E.R.BARMAY
    Wiley, 1958

SURVIVAL OF HUMAN PATHOGENS IN COMPOSTED SEWAGE
    Wiley & Westerberg
    Applied Microbiology, Dec.69, pp994-1001.

WATER BIBLIOGRAPHY (see also WIND section)

BRITISH WATERMILLS
    Leslie Syson
    Batsford, 1964

DESIGN, CONSTRUCTION AND MAINTENANCE OF EARTH
    DAMS AND EXCAVATED PONDS
    Forest Records, No.75
    H.M.S.O., London, 1971

DISCOVERING WATERMILLS
    J.N.T.Vince
    Shire, 1970

GRAVITY
    George Gamow
    Doubleday-Anchor, 1962

HYDROELECTRIC ENGINEERING PRACTICES
    J.G.Brown
    Blackie, 1958

HYDRO-ELECTRIC HANDBOOK
    W.P.Creager & J.D.Justin
    Wiley, 1950

POWER FROM WATER
    T.A.L.Paton & J.G.Brown
    Leonard Hill, 1961

TIDAL POWER
    T.J.Gray & O.K.Gashus
    Plenum, 1972

TIDEMILLS
    Rex Wailes
    London Society for the Protection of
        Ancient Buildings, London 1957

WATER BIBLIOGRAPHY, Cont.

TIDEMILLS IN ENGLAND AND WALES
    Transactions of the Newcome Society 16
    1-33, 1935-6

WATERLIFTING DEVICES FOR IRRIGATION
    Agricultural Development Paper, No.60.
    F.A.O. Rome, 1956

WATER-MILLS WITH HORIZONTAL WHEELS
    P.N.WILSON
    Society for the Protection of Ancient
        Buildings, London, 1960

WATER PAPER MILLS IN ENGLAND
    R.A.Shorter
    Society for the Protection of Ancient
        Buildings, London, 1966

HEAT PUMP BIBLIOGRAPHY

ENGINEERING THERMODYNAMICS
    G.F.C.Rogers & T.R.Mathew
    Longmans, 1965

HEAT PUMPS AND ELECTRIC HEATING
    E.R.Ambrose
    Wiley, 1966

HEATING AND VENTILATING ENGINEERS' JOURNALS
        or
REFRIGERATING ENGINEERS' JOURNALS
    look up HEAT PUMPS in their index.

PUMPS MANUAL
    Trade and Technical Press Ltd.
    Morden, Surrey, U.K., 1964

STEAM BIBLIOGRAPHY

THE EFFICIENT USE OF STEAM
    Olive Lyle
    H.M.S.O., London, 1958

A PORTABLE POWER UNIT THAT LIVES ON THE LAND
    Bulletin No.3
    National Research & Development Council
    October 1954, 12pp.

THE RICARDO STEAM OPERATED PRIME MOVER
    Technical Memo, 1 Jan. 1953
    National Research & Development Council

STEAM CARS, 1770-1970.
    Montagu & Bird
    Cassell, 1972

STEAM ENGINE THEORY AND PRACTICE
    William Ripper
    Longmans, 1922
    500pp.

STEAM PLANT FOR THE 1970'S
    Convention Proceedings
    Institute of Mechanical Engineers, 1969

STEAM.....general note: There are many other
books on STEAM in print at any time.....too
many to list more than a brief selection here.
You can look others up in either BRITISH BOOKS
IN PRINT (Whitaker) or in BOOKS IN PRINT pub.
by BOWKER, for American titles.

GEOTHERMAL BIBLIOGRAPHY

(Publisher's note: GEOTHERMAL information is generally very hard to obtain. For such an obvious source of energy, literally beneath your feet, there is surprisingly little fact. In addition to the books below, try the Library, Commercial Attache or the Science Attache of any of the following Embassies: JAPAN, ITALY, NEW ZEALAND or ICELAND.)

MINERAL AND THERMAL WATERS OF THE UNITED KINGDOM
    W.M.Edmunds et al.
      Part of MINERAL AND THERMAL WATERS OF THE WORLD
          A REPORT OF THE 23rd SESSION OF THE
          INTERNATIONAL GEOLOGICAL CONGRESS
    Prague, 1968.
    (One of the best references.)

NEW SOURCES OF ENERGY
    United Nations, 1964
    Vols. 2 and 3.

TERRESTRIAL HEAT FLOW IN ENGLAND
    E.C.Bullard and E.R.Niblett
    M.N.R.A.S., 1951
    (Nottinghamshire & Yorkshire)

TERRESTRIAL HEAT FLOW IN GREAT BRITAIN
    A.E.Benfield
    Proceedings of the Royal Society
    London, 1939

THERMAL ENERGY FROM THE EARTH'S CRUST
    C.J.Bawell
    New Zealand Journal of Geology & Geophysics, 6
    pp.52-69.
    Intro. and Part 1.

THERMAL SPRINGS OF THE U.S. AND OTHER COUNTRIES OF
    THE WORLD
    G.A.Waring
    Prof. paper of the U.S.Geological Survey, 492.
    1965
    383pp.

MISCELLANEOUS BIBLIOGRAPHY

CALOR GAS STOCKIST LIST
    Calor Gas House
    West Slough, Bucks., U.K.

ECOLOGICAL ENERGETICS
    John Phillipson
    Arnold, 1970

THE EFFICIENT USE OF FUEL
    H.M.S.O., LONDON, 1959

ELECTRICITY WITHOUT DYNAMOS
    J.W.Gardner
    Pelican

ENERGY CONVERSION JOURNAL
    Pergamon Press

ELECTRICITY SUPPLY REGULATIONS
    H.M.S.O., London, 1937

THE FOXFIRE BOOK
    Eliot Wigginton, ed.
    Anchor, 1972
    (See especially the Chapter on Alcohol Stills)

MISCELLANEOUS BIBLIOGRAPHY, Cont.

HEAT ENGINES AND APPLIED HEAT
    F.Metcalfe
    Cassell, London, 1969

TEACH YOURSELF HOUSEHOLD ELECTRICITY
    E.U.P., U.K.

HYDROGEN PRODUCTION HOMEMADE FUEL
    Science Mag., 22 Oct.71, pp174 & 367

MECHANICAL AIDS TO SMALLHOLDING
    D. DeSaulles
    Pearson, 1955

THE PNEUMATIC HANDBOOK
    British Compressed Air Society
    Trade and Technical Press, U.K., £5.25

PROSPECTS OF THE STIRLING ENGINE FOR VEHICULAR
    PROPULSION
    R.J.Meijer
    Phillips Tech. Review Reprint, P.96
    N.V.Phillips
    Gloeilampenfabrieken, Eindhoven, Netherlands

SMALL SCALE POWER GENERATION (straight fuel)
    Department of Economics & Social Affairs
    No. 67.11.B.7.
    United Nations, 1967

THE STIRLING ENGINE
    Intermediate Technology Development Group
    London, 1972

A STUDY OF POWER GENERATION BASED ON THE
    UTILISATION OF LOW GRADE FUELS IN
    DEVELOPING COUNTRIES
    Sales No. E.69.11.B.11.
    United Nations, 1969

TURBINES, STEAM, WATER AND GAS
    Edgar T. Westbury
    Percival Marshall, 1964

UNCONVENTIONAL THERMAL, MECHANICAL, AND NUCLEAR
LOW POLLUTION POTENTIAL POWER SOURCES FOR URBAN
VEHICLES
    Society of Automotive Engineers, 1968,
    U.S.Publication.
    Includes a good short section on storage.

USE OF ENERGY STORAGE FOR UNCONVENTIONAL ENERGY
    SOURCES TO AID DEVELOPING COUNTRIES
    KenA.McCollom
    School of Electrical Engineering
    Oklahoma State University
    Stillwater, Oklahoma, U.S.A.

or, with linked thunder-bolts, |

This is where 'ENERGY' blows out into a hundred
other categories (Categories are illusion). From
a thousand books that could suggest new de-
limitations for the term, ENERGY, here are a few:

DIRECTORY OF HAND OPERATED AND ANIMAL DRAWN
    EQUIPMENT
    Intermediate Technology Development Group

THE DIVINING ROD
    Mullins et al.
    Mullins, Bath, U.K., 1927

DOWSING
    W.H.Trinder
    British Society of Dowsers, 1939

FARM HORSES
    Young Farmers Club Booklet, No.13.
    National Federation of Young Farmers Clubs
    Pilot Press, 1944

FINDING AND USING TECHNICAL INFORMATION
    R.J.P.Carey
    EDWARD ARNOLD, 1966

FIVE ELEMENTS OF ACUPUNCTURE AND CHINESE
    MASSAGE
    Lawson Wood
    Health Science Press, 1966

FOOT POWER LOOMS
    Leaflet No. 90
    Dryad
    Northgates, Leicester

THE GOLDEN BOUGH
    J.G.Frazer
    Macmillan, various dates and editions.

MAGIC, AN OCCULT PRIMER
    David Conway
    Jonathan Cape, London, 1972

THE NATURAL HISTORY OF THE VAMPIRE
    Anthony Masters
    Hart-Davis/MacGibbon, London, 1972

PSYCHIC DISCOVERIES BEHIND THE IRON CURTAIN
    Ostrander & Schroeder
    Abacus

RELIGION AND THE DECLINE OF MAGIC
    Keith Thomas
    Weidenfeld & Nocholson, London, 1971

J.B.RHINE
    Any books by.

THE ROOTS OF COINCIDENCE
    Arthur Koestler et al
    Hutchinson, London, 1973

SENSE-RELAXATION
    Gunther (Esalen Institute)
    Macdonald, 1969

THE SERPENT POWER
    John Woodroffe
    Ganesh & Co.
    Madras, India
    The basic work on Kundalini Yoga, which is the
        Yoga of Energy or Serpent Power.

SUPERSTITIONS ABOUT ANIMALS
    Frank Gibson
    Walter Scott, London, 1904

TAI-CHI
    Cheng Man-ch'ing and Robert W.Smith
    Charles Tuttle, 1967

THE TAROT
    Bill Butler
    Rider & Co., London, 1974

THE VIEW OVER ATLANTIS
    John Michell
    Garnstone Press, London, 1971
    (Also in paperback)

WATER DIVINING
    S.N.Pike
    Research Publications
    London 1945

WILLIAM REICH
    Any books by, particularly any references to
    the Orgone or to Orgone Accumulators.

ADDRESSES

Other addresses are included in the main part of
this bibliography or can be found in BOOKS IN PRINT
or BRITISH BOOKS IN PRINT. Information sources tend
to be widely spread out and very centralized; so
Specialist Institution Libraries may be best for
information. Due to the current explosion of
interest in the subject a diplomatic approach may
get you much useful assistance from overworked
library staff.

BRACE RESEARCH INSTITUTE
    (low cost technologies)
    McDonald College, McGill University
    Ste.Anne deBellevue 800
    Quebec, Canada

BRAD (Biotechnic Research and Development)
    Eithin-y-Gaer
    Churchstoke
    Montgomeryshire
    Send S.A.E...for information.

ELECTRICAL DEVELOPMENT ASSOCIATION a.k.a.
    ELECTRICITY MARKETING COUNCIL
    Trafalgar Buildings
    1, Charing Cross Road, London, S.W.1.

FOUNDATION FOR THE GENERATION OF ELECTRICITY BY
    WINDMILLS
    B.W.Colenbrander
    Jan Steenlaan, 12
    Heenstad
    Netherlands

HAROLD BATE
    Pennyrowden
    Blackawton
    Totnes
    Devon
    Harold Bate is the legendary Devon chicken-
    farmer who powers an automobile with bottled
    Propane Gas. He has additionally designed a
    Methane Motoring Kit which is available from

    SYDNEY, RUSSEL AND SONS
        Walsal, Staffordshire, England.

JOTUL SCANDINAVIAN WOODBURNING STOVES
    Imported by BROBARTS LTD.
    12, Golden Square, Aberdeen, Scotland
    Apparently these are the only Woodburning
    Stoves available in Britain. 3 Sizes:
    No. 602 (3,000cu.f.--£25), No.118 (5,000cuf.
    £46) and No. 4 (up to 7,000 cu.f., £62)

ADDRESSES, Cont.

LOW IMPACT TECHNOLOGY, LTD.
    73, MOLESWORTH ST.
    Wadebridge, Cornwall
    Contact them for up to date commercial
    information, addresses etc.

PATENT OFFICE LIBRARY
    Good for Idea Generation.

RISING FREE COLLECTIVE
    197, Kings Cross Road
    London, W.C.1.
    Very useful for hard-to-find pamphlets.
    Agit-literature, library & distribution.

ST. GEORGE'S SCHOOL
    Wallesey, Cheshire, U.K.
    A Solar Heated School!

SOCIETY FOR THE PROTECTION OF ANCIENT BUILDINGS
    55, Great Ormond Street
    London, W.C.1.
    Produce a comprehensive booklist on Wind/
    Water/Tidal Power. Write for membership.

UPDATE ON SURVIVAL SCRAPBOOK/SHELTER & SURVIVAL
    SCRAPBOOK/FOOD.

Since SHELTER and FOOD were put together there
has been an explosion of information on similar
and related topics. Here are a few essential
additions:

THE ENGLISH GYPSY CARAVAN
    C.H.Ward-Jackson & Denise Harvey
    David & Charles, 1972

FOOD FOR FREE
    Richard Mabey
    Collins, 1972
    An amazing and useful book.

FREEDOM TO BUILD
    John Turner & Robert Fichter
    Macmillan, 1973

UPDATE ON SHELTER AND FOOD, Cont.

LEAF PROTEIN PROJECT
    Find Your Feet, Ltd., June 1972
    21, Wilsham Road
    Abingdon, Berkshire, U.K.

LOW-COST HOMES TO RENT OR BUY
    J.E.McKenzie Hall
    R.Hale, 1971

THE PATTERN OF ENGLISH BUILDING
    Alec. Clifton-Taylor
    Faber, London, 1972

PONDS AND FISH CULTURE
    C.B.Hall
    Faber, 1949

PRINCIPLES OF PNEUMATIC ARCHITECTURE
    R.N.Dent
    Architectural Press, London, 1973

SHELTERS, SHACKS AND SHANTIES
    Don Beard
    Pub. unknown. A review copy would be
    appreciated.

THE SOIL ASSOCIATION JOURNAL
    30p from Walnut Tree Manor
    Haughty, Stowmarket, Suffolk, U.K.

THE THATCHER'S CRAFT
    CoSIRA, 1961

THE WILDERNESS CABIN
    Calvin Rustrum
    Collier Macmillan, 1972

Any Bibliography or list of Addresses is only
as useful as the information in it is current
and relevant. The Editor would welcome
suggestions for further Addresses/Books, to be
included in further SURVIVAL SCRAPBOOKS or
to be passed on to people preparing similar
books elsewhere. Make Information **FREE**.